Profit for the Lord

Christian World Mission Books

Richard H. Drummond, *A History of Christianity in Japan*
Justo L. Gonzalez, *The Development of Christianity in the Latin Caribbean*
Stephen Neill, *The Story of the Christian Church in India and Pakistan*
Jane M. Sales, *The Planting of the Churches in South Africa*

R. Pierce Beaver, *All Loves Excelling*
Elizabeth Kelsey Kinnear, *She Sat Where They Sat: A Memoir of Anna Young Thompson*

Kenneth Strachan, *The Inescapable Calling*

William J. Danker, *Profit for the Lord*
A. Theodore Eastman, *Chosen and Sent: Calling the Church to Mission*
Donald C. Lord, *Mo Bradley and Thailand*
Paul B. Pedersen, *Batak Blood and Protestant Soul: The Development of National Batak Churches in North Sumatra*
David M. Stowe, *Ecumenicity and Evangelism*

R. Pierce Beaver, *To Advance the Gospel: The Collected Writings of Rufus Anderson*
R. Pierce Beaver, *Pioneers in Mission*
James A. Scherer, *Justinian Welz: Essays by an Early Prophet of Mission*
Max A. C. Warren, *To Apply the Gospel: Selections from the Writings of Henry Venn*

Profit for the Lord

*Economic Activities in Moravian Missions
and the Basel Mission Trading Company*

by

WILLIAM J. DANKER

William B. Eerdmans Publishing Company
Grand Rapids, Michigan

To my parents
and my wife
who have always sought
"profit for the Lord"

Editorial Foreword

It is common knowledge that through the centuries Christian missions exerted a powerful influence on the development or improvement of agriculture through teaching methods, introducing better stock and seeds (as well as new species), and setting an example for emulation. Some agricultural crafts were usually taught in connection with such work. Such activity, especially in the nineteenth century and early twentieth, was intended primarily to elevate the economic state of the people and make possible support of the church. Not since the secularization of the missions in Spanish America had missionary sponsored agriculture and ranching brought much income into support of the enterprise. Industrial schools were an early feature of Protestant missions, but lost favor and have been a minor activity. Industry for profit and trade for profit were usually considered to be incompatible with proclamation of the gospel. The Jesuit missionaries in Japan were bitterly attacked for participating in the silk trade, and two centuries later, for example, the great administrator and theoretician, Rufus Anderson, could not approve Cyrus Hamlin's business ventures in support of mission. English-speaking peoples know little or nothing about the large-scale economic activities of the Moravians and the Basel Evangelical Missionary Society in support of their missions and of what the practical consequences were.

Professor William J. Danker makes a notable contribution to mission history in this volume. His intention is also to stimulate churches and mission agencies to serious thinking about the possible role of economic programs in relation to mission action.

This book takes a significant place in the series "Mission Studies" in CHRISTIAN WORLD MISSION BOOKS. CWMB books treat mission history and theory, biography, and special studies in aspects of missiology. They are international and interdenominational in authorship.

R. Pierce Beaver
Editor

Contents

Preface   9

Part I

ECONOMIC ACTIVITIES IN A MISSIONARY CHURCH: THE MORAVIANS

I. Introduction   13

II. The Beginnings of a Missionary Church   16

III. Some Economic Attitudes and Activities in the
Life and Mission of the Brethren in Europe   20

IV. Economic Attitudes and Activities Among the
Brethren in Pennsylvania   25

V. A Moravian Missionary Principle: Profit for the Lord   31

VI. Economic Activities in the Mission to the Indians   38

VII. Economic Activities in Labrador   43

VIII. Economic Activities in Surinam   51

IX. Economic Activities in Africa   66

X. Balance Sheet on Moravian Economic
Activities for Missions   71

7

Part II

ECONOMIC ACTIVITIES AND A MISSION SOCIETY: THE BASEL MISSION TRADING COMPANY

XI.	Beginnings of the Basel Mission Society	79
XII.	Economic Activities in India	83
XIII.	Economic Activities in Africa	93
XIV.	Organization and Contributions of the Basel Enterprises	101
XV.	Separation of the Basel Mission Trading Company from the Mission Society	108
XVI.	Balance Sheet on the Basel Mission Trading Company	124
XVII.	Comparisons, Conclusions, and Implications	133
	Notes	143
	Bibliography	171
	Index	175

Abbreviations

EMM	*Evangelische Missions-Magazin*
EMZ	*Evangelische Missionszeitschrift*
RGG	*Religion in Geschichte und Gegenwart*

Preface

Today the whole relation of the Christian church to the secular realm stands front and center on the stage of world mission. As never before, the call goes out to the church to help men of all sorts and conditions to lead a more truly human life as the sons of God.

The disciple is challenged to help and befriend his neighbor in every bodily need, and to do this in the name of Christ. That function can scarcely be served without in some way helping him to improve and protect his livelihood.

In this age of nationalism churches must find their own indigenous economic basis. And they must be allowed the elbow room to devise not only their own structures for mission and ministry but also their own means to support them. Too long have western churches dictated both the games to be played as well as the rules by which to play them.

Western mission leaders and churchmen who demand that churches in the Third World operate entirely by the current western collection-plate economy may not be aware of the rich diversity of practice in their own past history represented by such missionary pioneers as the Unitas Fratrum, or Moravians, and the Basel Mission Trading Company.

It is the writer's hope that this study may not be only informative but liberating. Hopefully, it can help free Christians on mission frontiers in all six continents to find the forms that will carry out the tent-making mission of the church in the market place today.

Many a doctoral dissertation has been turned into a book. This manuscript started out to be a book, was turned into a doctoral dissertation at the University of Heidelberg, and a portion of it is herewith reconverted into a book.

Warm thanks for expert counsel go to Professor D. Hans-Werner Gensichen, my *Doktorvater,* and to Professor D. Heinrich Bornkamm, who served as *Koreferent* for the Heidelberg dissertation. R. Pierce Beaver, professor of missions at the Divinity School of the University of Chicago, has kindly lent counsel and critique on the basis of his encyclopedic knowledge of the Christian world mission. But any faults in this volume should, of course, be laid at the writer's door.

This study was facilitated by grants from the American Association of Theological Schools, the Aid Association for Lutherans, and the Wheat Ridge Foundation, which together provided the funds for two study trips to Europe. Without the warm interest of the administration and board of control of Concordia Seminary, St. Louis, this would not have come about.

Special recognition is due to the Reverend Vernon Nelson, who heads the Archives of the Moravian Church, Bethlehem, Pennsylvania; and to the Reverend Heinrich Bächtold, archivist of the Basel Mission Society. The Reverend Paul Theile of Switzerland, historian of the Moravian Church in Europe, and Dr. Jacques Rossel, Director of the Basel Mission Society, kindly read and corrected earlier drafts of this study.

And finally, it is a pleasure to express appreciation to a typist as cheerful as she is competent, Miss Lois Smith, and to Mr. Duane Bogenschneider and Mr. David Natzke who kindly read and corrected the manuscript.

William J. Danker

Part I

ECONOMIC ACTIVITIES IN
A MISSIONARY CHURCH:
THE MORAVIANS

I

Introduction

Protestant overseas missions in recent times have often demonstrated massive opposition to economic activities, particularly if these were intended to produce income. With uncritical piety, the axiom that the church (and therefore the mission) should have nothing to do with business has been widely accepted as a working presupposition. While mainline missions have often recognized the need for helping indigenous people achieve a livelihood, more fundamentalist missions have generally been extremely reluctant to divert energy or money from verbal proclamation of the gospel to social action.

Neither group has shown much interest in helping the national church, to say nothing of the mission, achieve an indigenous economic base. There are many so-called "independent" national churches in overseas mission fields, with impressive tables of organization, but to an overwhelming extent they remain financially dependent on western-based, western-funded denominational and ecumenical agencies. Western patterns of church and mission support have in practice become standard for non-western churches, however poorly these may fit the local culture and economic situation.

It was not always so. Early in the history of Protestant missions we find important missionary efforts taking a much more sympathetic view of economic activities. In some cases economic activities became the mainstay of missionary support; in others they provided significant assistance. While it was recognized that the main purpose of missions was to proclaim the gospel, it was also early recognized that a Christian missionary had an obligation to help and befriend his neighbor in every bodily need, including the need of a livelihood. Nor were these economic activities brief or spasmodic efforts that belong to long past history. In the significant instances we shall raise they continued for generations. One large-scale enterprise is still going strong after two centuries.

Comparatively little is known about these efforts, even by many who are otherwise well-read in the history of missions. This regrettable ignorance is due to the relatively few books dealing with this subject, especially in the English language. For the sake of the light these historic instances may shed on some of our contemporary problems, I have undertaken to lift out for closer examination and comparison the two most important Protestant examples of broad and sustained economic activity in missions, namely those carried on in connection with the so-called Unitas Fratrum, or Moravian Church, and the Basel Mission Society. Moravian missions arose hardly a quarter century after the first Protestant beginnings. It is useful to remind ourselves of their place in that historic succession. Bartholomäus Ziegenbalg and Heinrich Plütschau, Lutheran pioneers of the Danish-Halle mission, arrived in India in 1706. Not long after, in 1721, Hans Egede, a Lutheran pastor from Norway, went to Greenland. In 1732 the small refugee Moravian Church on the estate of Count Ludwig von Zinzendorf in Saxony embarked on a missionary career unique in Protestant annals. I propose to describe the significant role of economic activities in that mission outreach.

The Basel Mission Society, founded in 1815, proved to be the most significant single Protestant mission society on the Continent, at least in terms of the number of daughter societies it brought forth. These societies include the Berlin Mission Society founded in 1824, the Rhenish Mission Society of 1826, the North German Mission Society (Hamburg) of 1836, and the Lutheran Leipzig Mission Society founded in the same year.[1] At first Basel devoted itself entirely to training missionaries for service predominantly under English and Dutch societies. However, it soon began to move into foreign mission work on its own. After an abortive beginning in the Caucasus in southern Russia, its first permanent effort was directed at India in 1834, exactly a century after the first Moravian missionaries arrived in the West Indies. A Basel auxiliary, the Basel Mission Trading Company, operated industrial and commercial enterprises rivalling and in some aspects exceeding those of the Moravians.

After a description of the role of economic activities in the missionary outreach of each of these groups, I shall conclude with comparisons and suggest possible applications to the present mission scene.

II

The Beginnings of a Missionary Church

The broadest and most comprehensive early Protestant missionary program, sixty years before William Carey, and only twenty-six years after the Danish-Halle pioneers came to India, was that launched in 1732 by the Unitas Fratrum, or as it is better known, the Moravian Church. To this day the record it established in the eighteenth century in proportion to its numbers shines undimmed.

The Moravians were the first Protestants to put into practice the idea that the evangelization of the heathen is the duty of the church as such. Hitherto it had been a part of colonial policy, or had been espoused by missionary societies. It was this concept, carried out at the cost of blood, sweat, and tears, that made the Moravian mission so influential. No church better illustrates the total apostolate.

At the Ecumenical Missionary Conference of 1900 in New York, John R. Mott paid this tribute:

> The most striking example of achievement on the home field in the interest of foreign missions is that of the Moravians. They have done more in proportion to their ability than any other body of Christians.[1]

At that time in Protestant churches at large, the proportion of missionaries to members was about 1 to 5,000, but among the Moravians 1 to 60.[2] More recently, with increasing emphasis on indigenous workers, the proportion is 1 to 400.[3]

ORIGIN OF THE MORAVIAN CHURCH

The springboard for the Moravian world mission was a little village of six hundred people on the Berthelsdorf estate of Nikolaus Ludwig Count Zinzendorf, who had come under the pietistic, mission-minded influence of August Hermann Francke. The first Moravian refugees were received on his estate, and Herrnhut was founded almost without Zinzendorf's knowledge or help. He never really had the intention of settling them on his property.[4]

However, Zinzendorf was only twenty-two at the time, and his pietistic grandmother, Henriette Catherine von Gersdorf, who had reared him, not only consented in his absence, but also indicated through the estate's overseer[5] the place where the refugees were to settle. The site of Herrnhut was swampy land at the foot of the Hutberg, clearly unsuitable for cultivation.[6] The first refugees were cutlers. And they built for each family a house by the side of the road.[7] By that road their customers would come to them, and by that same road they were called to shoulder their artisan's tools and follow the Lamb in a mission to all the world.

These Moravians were one remaining strand of reform efforts arising in the wake of the burning of John Hus in 1415. About 1458, a group of lay people who had been seeking to live as Christian brethren decided to take the Bible as the rule for doctrinal questions and as the pattern for the renewal of the apostolic church. Originally they had called themselves the *fratres legis Christi,* later *Unitas Fratrum.* They also had certain roots in the Eastern Church.[8] They were persecuted frequently, but most severely through the Thirty Years' War and the Counter-Reformation. It was a small group of German-speaking Moravians[9] who fled to Saxony and found refuge on Zinzendorf's estate, where they formed a spiritually and economically integrated community.

BEGINNINGS IN OVERSEAS MISSIONS

At the court of the Danish king in Copenhagen, which was remarkably sympathetic to Pietism, the trails of three noted early efforts in Protestant missions crossed. The Danish-Halle missionaries Bartholomäus Ziegenbalg and Heinrich Plütschau were sent to India in 1706 by the Danish crown, as one of the few Protestant examples to match the mission zeal of the Catholic kings of Spain and Portugal.

Hans Egede, pioneer missionary to Greenland, would have been helpless when the company of merchants in Bergen withdrew their support had it not been for the ongoing, though occasionally faltering, support of the Danish king.

Count Ludwig von Zinzendorf, protector and later bishop of the Unitas Fratrum, was a scion of Europe's very highest aristocracy. As a cousin by marriage of the Danish king, Zinzendorf arrived in Copenhagen on May 12, 1731, to attend the coronation of Christian VI. On that occasion he saw several men from the western hemisphere who gave him the immediate impetus to realize his long-cherished dream of missions to the heathen. This encounter gave him "the handle by which to take hold of it," as Zinzendorf later said.[10] Two stalwart Herrnhuters, David Nitschmann and Leonhard Dober, accompanied Zinzendorf. His acquaintance with Count Ferdinand Danneskjold Laurvig, a member of the royal court who had been in St. Thomas, led him into conversation with the Count's valet, a Negro slave from the West Indies named Anton Ulrich, who told Zinzendorf heart-rending tales of the spiritual and physical misery of slaves on his home island of St. Thomas.[11] At about the same time, Zinzendorf and his two zealous companions also met two Greenland Eskimos whom Egede had sent; and they heard with sorrow that the government intended to give up the difficult mission in Greenland.[12]

How had Zinzendorf come by his dream of world missions? As mission interest frequently does, it had started very early in life. Zinzendorf's relatives had enrolled him at the age of ten in the Paedagogium at Halle, where he was exposed to accounts of the East India mission begun only four years earlier. Here he also met Plütschau, who visited Halle in November 1713. In autumn of 1715, Ziegenbalg came from India to Halle and married the sister of Zinzendorf's friend Salzmann. These personal encounters with the heroic India pioneers at Halle must have made a profound impression on young Zinzendorf.[13] At Halle Zinzendorf also lived and studied amid August Hermann Francke's great complex of charitable institutions and business enterprises. This Christian entrepreneur managed to support his community of institutions not only through a widespread network of collections, but also by means of business enterprises, including publishing houses and a drug store. These enterprises exhibited excellent administration and tireless pietistic zeal to work. Francke knew how to combine faith and calculation, Christian shrewdness and true piety in a masterful fashion.[14]

This example was not lost on the impressionable and imaginative youth. It helped shape the intimate connection between mission and economics that was to characterize the witness of Zinzendorf and the Moravians.

Halle inspired him with a dream. Herrnhut and its Moravian refugees provided him with the people—the *gens aeterna* over whose readiness to witness and to die he marvelled at St. Thomas.[15] And Copenhagen gave Zinzendorf the opening to begin.

III

Some Economic Attitudes and Activities
in the Life and Mission
of the Brethren in Europe

It will be of interest to describe some of the economic attitudes of the Brethren as well as the economic activities which were in part both their result and their cause. Although private property continued, the spiritual unity of the Brethren was expressed in various communal economic enterprises: a credit union, the growing and spinning of flax, a salt monopoly (which returned substantial profits), beer brewing (which led to difficulties when a tavern was established), and an apothecary's shop. Every effort was made to help each member earn the necessary income, while at the same time frustrating every attempt at personal enrichment or private exploitation.

These early years at Herrnhut were of formative influence in providing the spiritual and economic basis for its remarkable missionary accomplishments. Otto Uttendörfer maintains that the spirit developed during these early years—the spirit of sacrifice and of being content with little for oneself while devoting much to the Lord's cause—is the secret of later Moravian accomplishments.[1]

Since Count Zinzendorf faced great needs, but was as impractical in financial matters as he was aristocratic in blood, the Unitas Fratrum repeatedly found itself in economic crisis. In 1753, during Zinzendorf's years in England, his chronic fiscal embarrassment reached such a pitch that the Count escaped debtor's prison in London by a matter of hours.[2] In view of this, it is natural that many schemes were proposed to provide additional income.

When plans were advanced to organize a trading society to win profits for the Savior's cause, they apparently ran aground on the prejudices of Zinzendorf's landed class.[3] Zinzendorf, as a member of the top layer of European aristocracy, shared the general prejudices of his class against trade and commerce.[4] He identified himself as a feudal aristocrat and ruled with benevolent paternalism. He did not see himself as a member of the emerging class of capitalists.[5] His Lutheran background also biased him against trade.[6]

The Count's attitude toward community-owned enterprises was somewhat ambiguous. On the one hand he expressed verbal opposition to them:

Trade and commerce, shops and stores, are not befitting to our communities, they should be left to private individuals and partnerships. All professions and commercial transactions from which a community profits give the semblance of a *communio bonorum* and are therefore an abomination in the eyes of the ecclesiastical ordinary. Furthermore they make it necessary for a community as community to borrow more and more capital and to become enmeshed in monetary transactions and market situations.[7]

On the other hand, some communal enterprises produced profits which helped pay some of the rising costs of Moravian missions.[8] At any rate, the Count's opposition was all too often not voiced until after the accomplished fact. If these were really matters of principle rather than prejudice, why did he not refuse to sell the general store and the drugstore to the community?[9]

Though the prejudices of his class often inhibited economic development, the noble Count could on occasion give beautiful expression to the modern insight that in social no less than in architectural structures, form must follow function:

Our economic systems cannot maintain the same course for more than a generation. They may well conserve themselves, so as not to perish. But they must be capable of being poured into as many different molds as it pleases the Savior for aeons on end.[10]

Three years later Zinzendorf again demonstrated that his genius had grasped one of the basic principles of modern administration, namely its concern for leading a corporate structure, whatever its nature, to carry out its own continuing change: "I have observed that the preservation of the community is best assured through a process of continuous change."[11] At the same time, Zinzendorf's stance toward the establishment of industries among the Brethren hardly kept pace with the tempo of economic change. As early as 1746, he opposed industries because he wanted no profiteering in the Savior's name.[12]

But Zinzendorf's chief criterion for any economic system was this: Will it help or hinder the function of mission? If it inhibited the missionary mobility of his elite Moravian shock troops, he was against it, whatever it was. For the very same basic reason he could oppose both the time-honored livelihood of agriculture and the brand-new system of factory work. Both tied the worker down and interfered with the freedom of movement and independence of action which best promoted his missionary effectiveness.[13]

Commerce and trade would appear to have been more compatible with missionary mobility than either agriculture or factory work. Yet several factors militated against easy acceptance of this economic pursuit. Count Zinzendorf's instinctive aristocratic distaste for trade was paralleled by the prejudices which the first Moravian settlers brought with them to Herrnhut.[14]

They were reinforced in their scruples by converts like August Gottlieb Spangenberg, a theologian who had studied at Jena and had been professor at Halle.[15] He felt that trade was just as harmful to the human soul as slaveholding.[16]

In time, the need to support their far-flung missions drove the Moravians to strenuously re-think their traditional bias against trade.[17] Later, the Moravian mission in Labrador came to be supported entirely by the income from trade with the Eskimos. The English Moravians even owned their own ships, in which they carried on the Labrador trade for a century and a half, as we shall see.[18]

The Moravians found strong and growing support at home through the work of Abraham Dürninger, a merchant genius who had found in Herrnhut a congenial spiritual home.[19] In 1747 Zinzendorf placed the little general store in Herrnhut under the management of the new Brother, a forty-one-year-old experienced merchant.[20] Over the next twenty-five years Dürninger made over to the Unitas Fratrum a total of 131,715 talers for its purposes at home and abroad.[21] Besides, the store and its related businesses gave employment to many Brethren and enabled them to contribute to the treasury of the Brethren and the missions they supported.[22] Under Dürninger's skillful and devoted hands the little general store grew to an international business complex in textiles, especially linen,[23] tobacco, and the wholesale and retail trade, manufacturing and export-import business.[24]

When Dürninger took over the community store in 1747, it had debts totaling 651 talers, although the goods in stock were valued at 2,856 talers.[25] At the time of his death, his company had a capital of 277,000 talers and owned buildings worth a total of 39,000 talers.[26] The firm's profits at the time of Dürninger's death were about 15% annually. In addition, Dürninger had during his lifetime contributed to Herrnhut, the Unitas Fratrum, and its various missionary efforts a total of 131,914 talers.[27] By 1800 the net annual profits almost doubled the best year of the founder, reaching 100,000 talers.[28] And the enterprise Dürninger so dramatically expanded, maintained itself through the vicissitudes of the next two centuries.[29]

Other promising Moravian business enterprises in both Herrnhut and overseas might have prospered even more had they, like Dürninger, understood the importance of capital formation. Most Moravians urged that all profits could best advance the cause of the Lamb by being devoted directly to missionary activities. Dürninger's keen business mind alone saw that if some of the profits were ploughed back into the business, they could then multiply financial support for missions in the future. But he was ahead of his time.

Tensions between missions and economic activities are apparent in Dürninger's career. The need for organizational separation was immediately clear to this shrewd businessman. He allowed the business to bear his own name so as to distinguish it from the Unitas Fratrum, which was for decades in desperate financial straits because of Zinzendorf's lack of financial realism. Whatever the Unity's credit standing, Dürninger's rating remained good, thanks to this arrangement.[30]

While the Dürninger firm served the mission, missions did not always advance the business. He complained that he could not run a business if his best weavers were taken from him on one day's notice to go abroad as missionaries. He had little use for the lot as a method of reaching decisions that affected the business, and on at least one occasion, when a valued employee had been chosen by the lot for missionary service, Dürninger managed to have the verdict of the lot reversed.[31]

Dürninger's connection with Herrnhut was at best a dubious business asset. Not only did it fail to help his credit, but its people, as they became familiar with the pietistic aristocrats who frequented Herrnhut, became too demanding. In spite of his genuine desire to provide employment for the Brethren, Dürninger was forced to recruit about 75% of his employees from outside communities to get people willing to work for the wages he offered. Only in this way could he make any profits for the community and for its missions.[32] Gillian Lindt Gollin contends:

> Dürninger himself has all too often been portrayed as the Christian capitalist par excellence, as though his Christianity somehow made him a better businessman. In fact, however, it is clear that Dürninger's firm would have prospered even further and developed far more rapidly had it not been for his bent toward religious mysticism and the partiality he showed to the religious and social goals of Herrnhut.[33]

However, she fails to appreciate that maximum business profit was not the highest value either of Dürninger or his admiring biographers, Herbert Hammer and Hans Wagner. It is valid to call Dürninger an ideal Christian entrepreneur, precisely because he did not regard business as an end in itself, but subordinated it to the ultimate goals of his faith.

The Moravian settlements in England had their own industries and other occupations.[34] The brethren found it convenient and helpful to live in such warmhearted communities offering a total way of life and an attractive fellowship such as were to be found nowhere else.[35] Though John Wesley, in spite of his early spiritual debt to the Moravians, carried on a running battle with Zinzendorf and with Moravian doctrine for at least two decades, he paid this high tribute to the English settlements for their wise use of mammon:

> you are not slothful in Business, but labour to eat your own Bread; and wisely manage the Mammon of Unrighteousness, that ye may have to give to others also, to feed the Hungry, and cover the Naked with a Garment.[36]

IV

Economic Attitudes and Activities
Among the Brethren in Pennsylvania

Also in the New World the economic communalism of the Moravians was richly developed. It was a communism not of goods, but of labor, as Edmund de Schweinitz has neatly distinguished. Those who had private property kept it. But no one worked for himself, or carried on business of his own. All gave their time and labor to the Church. In return, they received the necessities of life from the Church.[1] Centering at their chief colony in Bethlehem,[2] Pennsylvania, the Moravians organized their so-called "General Economy," which embraced all the trades and industries as well as personnel of the Brethren at Bethlehem, including a number of neighboring agricultural settlements, notably Nazareth, Gnadenthal, Christiansbrunn, and Friedensthal. The foundation of the General Economy consisted of over 6000 acres of land purchased between 1741 and 1749.[3]

The General Economy became a beehive of activity, and in pre-Revolutionary Pennsylvania a craft center of no mean significance. The Brethren were clothed with textiles their own hands and machines had woven, among them no less than eleven qualities of linen.[4] Outsiders eagerly sought the products of their large pottery at standard prices.[5] Their brewery was able to supply not only the Brethren but also their neighbors with plenty of good beer. The tannery, whose 200-year-old vats were excavated in 1966, was particularly profitable.[6] Faithfulness, service, and system are the basic principles in every endeavor, even down to shoe-shining.[7]

One reason why Bethlehem enjoyed greater prosperity than Herrnhut lay in the agricultural base it had and Herrnhut did not.[8] Still another factor was Bethlehem's lower overhead costs for administrative personnel. Both in absolute terms and proportionately, their number was considerably fewer than in Herrnhut.[9] Moreover, during the General Economy from 1742 to 1762, Bethlehem had virtually no unskilled workers, while in Herrnhut at this time they formed 10 per cent of male workers and 18 per cent of the total labor force.[10]

But aside from crafts, the potential of Bethlehem for large-scale industry was not developed during pre-Revolutionary War days. Why not? Why did no Abraham Dürninger arise in Pennsylvania? The answer to the question is found in British law, which forbade the colonies to engage in manufacturing on any large scale.[11] Therefore Bethlehem had to be content with a busy and productive agricultural and craft economy.

Yet Bethlehem was more than a diligent ant colony. Rejecting the grim pietism of Halle, the Moravians celebrated their joyous life with the Lamb. Erich Beyreuther says, "It would be hard to find a happier congregation, or one in which there was more singing and music."[12]

Music was an ideal and harmonious expression of the social aspect of the Christian faith which Zinzendorf emphasized. Pietism is frequently labeled individualistic. But this adjective does not readily fit the Moravians. Zinzendorf was profoundly concerned about the social dimensions of the Christian life. He was not ready to acknowledge as Christian "a man who sees his goal in the Savior, but does not recognize His bride and knows nothing of His family."[13] Gillian Gollin correctly identifies a theological factor in the success of the Bethlehem communal economy. The Moravian subordinated his own interests to those of the community because he believed that the true Christian sees himself as a part of the family of God and must love not only God but his neighbor.[14] This communal love found frequent liturgical expression, including a ritual known as "love feasts," which were based on the practice of the primitive church. The beginning or the completion of any large economic activity, such as the clearing of a new field, or plowing or harvest, was generally observed with such a love feast. This consisted of hymn singing and liturgy, during which a simple meal such as coffee and bread or rolls was eaten together.

The General Economy was well suited to its time and place. It was very useful in warding off Indian attacks. And it was remarkably helpful to a group of immigrants in getting a foothold in a strange land. The Brethren needed each other on both counts.

For the first twenty years after its founding in 1742, Bethlehem had a thoroughly communal economy. Even the meals were taken together, instead of by families.[15] Josef L. Hromadka, in speaking of the relation between church and world observes: "Within the Reformation movement the Unitas Fratrum occupies a special place of its own and has in many respects anticipated the questions of today."[16] However, it must be remembered that there was no purpose of social revolution in the communal enterprises of the Brethren. They were adopted because they implemented spiritual objectives, especially the mission to the heathen. Interestingly, while Russian Communism has an avowed program of moving through socialism (perhaps more accurately, state capitalism) to pure communism, the Bethlehem Moravians moved in the opposite direction. After twenty years of pure communism, they dropped back to socialism, and eventually assimilated themselves to the surrounding capitalistic culture. In other overseas mission settlements communalism survived much longer. It is important to remember that Bethlehem was not really unique. Zinzendorf warned all Herrnhut missionaries against seeking personal profit. Community of goods without favoritism was expected of all Moravian missionaries.[17]

There was no Berlin wall around Bethlehem.[18] Expulsion, on the other hand, was a real danger. If an individual's way of life did not conform to good moral principles in general and the Herrnhut pattern in particular, he could be and often was summarily sent away.[19]

It was not only mutual economic support, or mutual protection against Indians and white persecutors that motivated the communalism of the General Economy. The smith at his roaring forge, the farmer in the hot haymow, the weaver at his monotonous loom, and even the brewer with his yeasting foam could wipe the sweat from their brows with more good will than otherwise might have been the case. They knew that their labors at Bethlehem and Nazareth were part of a general Moravian mission effort supporting missionary endeavors in the West Indies, Nicaragua, Greenland, Surinam, South America, among North American Indians, in South Africa, Persia,

Ceylon, Egypt, Algiers, the Gold Coast, and among the Jews.[20] One historian records:

> Two groups were formed, one to go into the forests as teachers and evangelists, the other to stay in the settlements to earn support for those who went out. Of the four hundred inhabitants in 1747, fifty-six were "absent in the service of the church."[21]

While almost all ecclesiastics and laymen of Europe's great churches ignored their world missionary obligations, the perspiring Moravian craftsman was supporting a worldwide embassy. And if the heavy burden of maintaining the community and supporting the missions to the Indians and the missions abroad encouraged individualistic tendencies among them, this would be perfectly natural and detracts nothing from their achievement. But it could hardly have been the dominant motive, for even after the dissolution of the General Economy, the Moravians of Bethlehem continued to give sacrificially for missions.

It was above all this mission concern that distinguished the Moravian colonies from those of the Amish or the modern Hutterites. The latter wished chiefly to flee from a wicked world, while the followers of Zinzendorf sought to develop economic bases to sustain a communal life independent of non-Moravian tendencies and to support a large number of missionaries.

The same artisans who were the mainstay of the communal economy were also the source of missionary volunteers. What was more natural than that where possible they should continue their crafts overseas rather than rely wholly on the over-strained exchequer of the tiny supporting groups? When these missionaries returned to the Moravian communities to report or to confer, they naturally continued to ply their trade. "Tent-making" came naturally to the Moravians, as it has never quite come to university- or seminary-trained missionaries.

Financially, the General Economy died not of failure but of success. With rising prosperity, individual instincts to have, to hold, and to spend according to one's own desire reasserted themselves.[22] Moreover, the individual family could not forever be content with the Chinese-commune-style dwelling units segregated by age and sex.

With the rise of prosperity and the departure from the General Economy, there was a general decline in willingness to work for the community as a whole. Religion became segregated from the realm of economics. Secularism was on the increase. Dissatisfaction had arisen already during the days of the General Economy when a diminishing proportion of craftsmen at Bethlehem found themselves supporting not only the community but a growing number of missionaries. By 1759 the latter constituted 36 per cent of the entire male labor force![23]

In the earlier years artisans had taken turns in mission service, but as time went on, specialization and permanency came to be desirable for both areas of service, not only for economics as Gollin implies. [24] However, she may be right in identifying one cause of economic discontent in Bethlehem:

> The economically productive workers, therefore, found themselves in a situation in which they had to provide for the economic support of persons whose jobs they aspired to but could rarely attain.[25]

And it is entirely possible that the spiritual decline in Bethlehem was in part the result of draining away too large a proportion of the charismatic elite into missions,[26] a risk that few other Protestant churches have ever run.

The halfway house of socialism and exclusivism, which followed the General Economy in 1762 and prevailed for the next eighty years, resulted in lowered vitality and growth. [27]

The Brethren must often have looked back with some nostalgia to the more unified and integrated world of the General Economy. In that earlier age of the communism of labor, the Brethren had made no practical distinction between the church and the settlement, the secular and the sacred. All duties had been religious duties. The whole society was welded into a unity by their religion.[28] Bethlehem became secularized more rapidly than Herrnhut, where the conservative and pious aristocracy played a key role in slowing the process down.[29] Ironically, the process of secularization had been promoted by the very missionary goals of the Moravians and of their commerce. For missions exposed them to the values of others,[30] and commerce and economic activities also opened them to the world.

The Moravians proved no exception to the curious inverse relation between religion (and therefore also missionary zeal) and

riches that John Wesley noted in a quotation given wide currency by
Max Weber and cited by Gollin:

> I fear that wherever riches have increased, the essence of
> religion has decreased in the same proportion. Therefore, I do
> not see how it is possible, in the nature of things, for any
> revival of true religion to continue long. For religion must of
> necessity produce both industry and frugality, and these
> cannot but produce riches. But as riches increase, so will pride,
> anger, and love of the world in all its branches.[31]

But the effect of prosperity on religious fervor and mission
performance in the case of the Moravians was not nearly so adverse
as among many other Protestants. The Moravian Church had early
reached a vastly higher plateau of integration of missions with
economic activities. If economic activities were a secularizing factor,
they also enabled the Moravians for over two centuries to support a
much higher proportion of missionaries than the average denomination. As a matter of fact, the process of secularization among
Moravians was not nearly so rapid as among other Protestants who
were often caught up one by one in the maw of modern
secularization without the protective hull of a close, interdependent
religious community embracing even economic matters.

V

A Moravian Missionary Principle:
Profit for the Lord

In 1732, David Nitschmann and Leonhard Dober became the first
Moravian missionaries when they established a mission to African
slaves on the isle of St. Thomas. Nitschmann supported both men by
carpentry. They were soon followed by other missionaries who
sought to support themselves by "secular" occupations, although it
is doubtful whether a good Moravian, especially in those days,
considered anything in God's world to be "secular."

Some became involved in colonization, on at least one occasion
with disastrous results. In 1734, at the invitation of Count Pless,
First Chamberlain at the Danish Court, eighteen Brethren went out
to serve on St. Croix as overseers of his plantations and as
missionaries at the same time. But they arrived there in a weakened
condition because of a long and difficult roundabout trip of more
than half a year. In the tropics the ship had run out of drinking
water, and scurvy had broken out. Three died already within weeks
after arriving at St. Thomas,[1] and before they had been much longer
on this rank and dank West Indies isle, most of them had died of
fever.[2] Though many mission histories dealing with the subject
speak of these missionaries' serving as "plantation overseers," there
were actually no plantations as yet! And this is just the point. On
St. Croix the "plantations" had not even been surveyed yet by the
government.[3] With the greatest difficulty the colonists had to press
into the primeval jungle and attempt to erect a temporary shelter

31

and plant gardens.[4] Under these circumstances, it is not surprising that the venture ended so tragically. But this sad episode can hardly be used as an argument to demonstrate that the basic principle of sending self-supporting missionaries was unsound. It rather demonstrates an ignorance of conditions overseas, poor preparation, and an unrealistic enthusiasm.

Zinzendorf, incidentally, was not enthusiastic about combining missions with colonization.[5] Perhaps he feared that a brother would not have the freedom necessary for his missionary duty if he were someone else's fulltime employee rather than a free artisan who could manage his own time to a much greater degree.

The Moravians not only approved but also expected and regulated self-support on the part of their missionaries. This was simply an extension of their domestic practice. At the urging of the Count, the seasonally unemployed of Herrnhut would go out in pairs and witness to the gospel, earning their living as they went.[6] Herrnhut had many artisans. For example, by 1747 there were no less than twenty-four shoemakers, one for every thirty-five people in the community. The surplus of artisans must have provided a ready pool of missionary recruits. One historian suggests that Zinzendorf also exported to the mission field those who were a threat to his personal supremacy because they criticized his allegedly deceptive Lutheranizing of the Unitas Fratrum.[7]

Even had the Unity been able to support its early missionaries by sending them money from the home churches, Zinzendorf would not have permitted it. And here the Count was thinking not of saving money for the sending church but of promoting the welfare of the people to whom the missionaries were sent. The missionaries should earn their own living, first, in order to teach the people the dignity of labor.[8] Next, they should do it for their own good.

Zinzendorf held strong opinions on the necessity of work. In a testament written for the Brethren before his first journey to the New World he wrote: "One works not only to live, but only lives for the sake of work; and if one no longer has work, one gets sick and dies."[9] The Count himself was an indefatigable worker and he believed with St. Paul that Christians must work "so that they may not become a burden to others but have something to give to the needy."[10] There was an essential place in the life of a Moravian Christian for the virtues of diligence, thrift, punctuality, and conscientious attention to detail,[11] all of them qualities useful for economic success. While Zinzendorf may have been prejudiced against commerce, he had no onesidedly spiritual conception of the life of the Brethren. He gave full recognition to the economic needs of the Unity. It was not easy to provide steady employment for the members of the congregation in all kinds of trades facing hard times amid the hatred of a surrounding world which would gladly have starved them out. Their frequent change of home and the constant work with souls complicated the economic problem. Officers of the congregation were to regard it as the object of very serious concern. He concludes, "They do not sin, if they plan ahead for this; they sin, if they neglect this duty."[12]

While the Count expected people to dedicate their lives to God's church and his mission, he was strangely reluctant to encourage regular giving to the treasuries of the church and its missions. Though the Moravians were exerting themselves heroically in sending forth missionaries, Zinzendorf was loath to publish their exploits. This differs sharply from the *Lettres Edifiantes* of the Jesuit missionaries. It also contrasts markedly with the *Hallesche Nachrichten* published by August Hermann Francke and the collection devices which the latter developed for his complex of charitable and religious projects at Halle. For a long time the letters and diaries of Moravian missionaries were restricted to private circulation chiefly in Moravian settlements.

Zinzendorf placed his entire fortune in the service of the Unitas Fratrum. And numerous aristocrats and other men of wealth followed his example by giving very large sums. But the Count was opposed in principle to collections. While he was very willing to receive whatever gifts were contributed voluntarily, he disliked appeals for aid and the gathering in of stated contributions. The chief reason he gave for his stand was that he did not think it right to interfere with those Christian causes which had existed prior to the renewal of the Unity, and which needed all the support they could get. Here we note the *noblesse oblige* attitude of the aristocrat; he may have intended here to avoid anything that could jeopardize the attainment of official respectability by his curious ecclesiastical hybrid. One instance of his strange aversion to church collections took place in Philadelphia in 1742. The Lutherans in that city had requested him to take temporary charge of their church, whose pulpit was vacant. During a solemn meeting to arrange the details of his interim pastorate, he put this astonishing question:

"Könnt ihr das Geben lassen?" ("Won't you stop giving?").[13] Of
course, he was a very blue-blooded count, and not a poor preacher
dependent on a salary. Only much later did regular missionary
offerings come about. Just as he supported himself at a proper
aristocratic level while serving the Lord, so he expected his followers
to support themselves in God's service at the level of their station in
life, whatever it was.

A half-century after the first artisans went forth as witnesses to
gather "souls for the Lamb," in the recurring Moravian phrase,
missionaries of the Unitas Fratrum were still expected to support
themselves as much as possible by the labor of their own hands.
They were also to have a common household.[14] In 1840, more than
a century after the first artisan witnesses went forth, Moravian
missionaries were instructed:

> The missionary should take a pleasure in saving or earning
> whatever he can, with propriety, on behalf of the mission in
> which he is employed, remembering that everything saved or
> earned is an advantage to the General Mission Fund, the claims
> upon which have become so numerous and so heavy.[15]

When the situation did not permit missionaries to earn their own
way they transmitted to the sending church a list of necessities,
which, if approved, were sent out to the field. The children and
widows were provided for.[16] At the same time, it was understood
that the missionary was not to carve out a kingdom for himself
overseas, but that all the profit of his so-called secular employment
was to accrue to the mission.[17] Both Zinzendorf and the Brethren
regarded the members of the Unity as a *militia Christi.*[18] And as
soldiers of Christ the Brethren were expected to seek profit for Jesus
Christ and not for themselves.

In the Moravians, Zinzendorf met an indestructible people in
whom he immediately recognized a special charisma of witnessing
to Jesus Christ. Under his inspiring leadership this gift was burnished
and heightened. He was not so much admonishing as describing the
Moravians when he said that the *militia Christi* "sacrifice food and
drink, sleep, necessities, their good name, time and energy and
everything." Thereby, he points out, they are only doing what
comes naturally:

> More concern for themselves would make them uneasy, but
> amid trouble and work they are happy and lighthearted. They

devote themselves to Christian witness "the way a fish swims or water makes wet." Nor do they regard this as any merit in themselves but are moved by the faithfulness and merit of Jesus Christ.

Zinzendorf contrasts Christ-centered militants with self-centered worldings:

> One says of certain people that they never fall off a bench without advantage to themselves. Militants know how to turn all external things, even the least, in such a way that they draw a certain profit out of them for their Lord, otherwise they refuse to get involved.[19]

This principle governed the choice of occupations. The occupation most compatible with witnessing was the artisan's life, and for this reason most of the early missionaries were expected to make their living in this way. As time went on, they developed into master craftsmen. And in places like St. Thomas they taught the slaves these trades, especially blacksmithing and shoemaking. These two crafts were preferred to bricklaying and carpentry, which often required the missionaries to be absent from their stations, or worse, forced them to use slaves as helpers at the plantations.[20]

Sex and marriage were subordinated to the fighter's cause. Zinzendorf impressed on the Moravians the ideal of the "Streiter-Ehe." Such marriages were dedicated to higher goals than a rising standard of consumption. Before marriage there was strict, almost monastic separation of the sexes. But in marriage sexual relations were to be accorded as much respect as birth and death.[21] The love life of husband and wife was seen as a symbol of the soul's relation to its Heavenly Bridegroom.

The refusal to get involved where there was no profit to be gained by way of winning souls explains the attitude of Zinzendorf and the Moravians towards slavery in the West Indies.[22] The Count was emphatic in his disapproval when the Brethren on St. Thomas began to teach the slaves to write. He pointed out, "One can anger the government by such small matters, and witnesses who use common sense will not do this."[23] As a small group on the margin of respectability and orthodoxy the Brethren were in no position to hazard their main mission of "winning souls for the Lamb" by engaging in such side-efforts as the direct educational uplift of the slaves in defiance of the slaveholders.

Almost half a century later, Bishop Spangenberg echoes these same sentiments, pointing out that European planters and traders feared both for their business and their lives, if the slaves learned to read and write. With Negroes outnumbering whites 100 to 1 on St. Thomas, how could white men be safe from rebellion, if the Negroes became better educated?[24] Spangenberg says, "One cannot deny that there is something to these statements." Therefore, he goes on, the Brethren adopted the principle of working for heartfelt conversions to Jesus. "In this way the people will become not only smarter but better." Those who have a mere head knowledge of Christianity can be dangerous. Long experience had only confirmed the Brethren in these ideas.[25] At another place, however, Spangenberg recognizes that the mere proclamation of the Christian doctrine already educates the heathen and runs the risk of interfering with present commercial and political dealings with them.[26]

But Spangenberg's caution was only in the interest of missions. Personally he abominated slavery and regarded it as "so inhuman that it makes your hair stand on end."[27] The Moravians were always motivated by what they considered best for the mission. When hostile slaveholders refused them access to the slaves on their plantations, the Brethren countered by purchasing plantations of their own complete with slaves, and evangelized them without the customary hindrances. The fact that their slaves were also better treated is evidenced by the fact that they stood by the Moravians when slave insurrections broke out.[28] And for all his apparent peace with the status quo, Zinzendorf did purchase the freedom of a black eldress in the Brethren Church on St. Thomas. No doubt, this was done to give her more freedom of movement and more time for her responsible work in the congregation.[29] The missionaries soon recognized, however, that owning and supervising slaves involved them in an ambiguous and contradictory situation.

As time went on, economic activities were put into the hands of specialized missionaries. The Labrador trade was committed to certain men sent out by the Moravian board expressly for that purpose. In St. Thomas, Surinam, Nicaragua, and South Africa in the latter half of the nineteenth century, unordained missionaries devoted themselves to trade and commerce, and yet also assisted in evangelistic work.[30]

The amount of income derived from "traffic and trade" was extraordinary. By 1882 about $100,000 per year was raised on the far-flung Moravian mission fields, a small amount by the contributions of native Christians, most of it by industry and trade.[31] One hundred thousand dollars was no small sum in those days, especially in the hands of thrifty Moravians.

VI

Economic Activities in the Mission to the Indians

David Zeisberger, the great Moravian missionary to the Indians, demonstrates in his missionary methods a ministry to the whole man. Coming as he did from Moravian settlements like Bethlehem and Nazareth, with their integration of the sacred and the secular into one total Christian life, it was perhaps only natural that he should attempt to create the same kind of community among the Indians. One cannot say that this was another example of Europeanism, foisting alien cultural patterns on the Indians. The Moravians were not primarily concerned about changing the aborigine's economic way of life. They rather urged their converts to practice their ancient ways of livelihood, but to do it with diligence—to plant, hunt, and fish at the right times, to prepare food for winter, etc. They taught the Greenlanders to keep their herring dry and unspoiled, and the Indians to cultivate their corn, so that when others lacked food, the convert would always have enough for himself and to help others.[1]

Nor was the religious communalism of the Moravians an instance of Europeanism, for it was not typical of European civilization at that time. Rather, it was one of the reasons why the Brethren were looked upon as curious heretics by most white settlers. Moravians and Indians shared the oppressive hostility of many whites. The spirit of the Moravian pattern must have made sense to the Indians, for their culture also found it natural that life should be a living whole. The ever-widening stream of white settlers doomed the hunting culture of the Indians, and the Moravians were only being realistic when they sought to substitute another type of economy and livelihood. Patiently, they taught the Indians agriculture and other arts and crafts of a settled mode of existence.[2] Unlike the Spanish and Portuguese in South America, most other whites in North America, with the exception of a handful of missionaries and their supporters, did not believe the Indian worth civilizing. At any rate, few of them took the trouble to teach him anything except the uses of gunpowder and cheap whiskey. Beginning in 1740, Christian Heinrich Rauch, the first Moravian missionary to the Indians, established prosperous villages of Christian Indians on the Herrnhut pattern at Shekomeko in Dutchess County, New York, and at Wechquadnach or Indian Pond on the New York-Connecticut border. Far from being pleased, the settlers were infuriated; they wanted the Indians eliminated.[3]

The American Indian received little from the white man except the encouragement to vanish. He had always been exposed to periodic starvation in his uncertain hunting culture. But for a few brief years and for a few hundred of his dwindling numbers he found a haven of peace and prosperity in Moravian Indian villages.[4] They give an indication of what might have been if white settlers in America had been as intent on the well-being of the Indian as they were on their own.

It is striking that within the present territorial limits of the United States the most promising early Protestant Indian mission work was that which most closely paralleled the approach of the Jesuits in Paraguay and Mexico. Zeisberger was as eager as the Jesuits in far-off Paraguay to protect his charges from his fellow whites. At Friedenshütten, a Christian Indian town in Bradford County, Pennsylvania, Zeisberger laid down the same regulation on the length of traders' visits which the Jesuits enforced: they were permitted to stay no more than two or three days at a time. Indians were forbidden by Zeisberger to get into debt with the traders or to receive goods on consignment from them. The liquor traffic was taboo. The converts promised obedience to their teachers and to the helpers appointed to preserve order in their meetings in the towns and fields.[5]

An idyllic picture of Friedenshütten, a Moravian Indian village, emerges from an early, firsthand report. The Indians lived in log houses with windows and chimneys like the homesteads of the settlers. The streets and alleys were kept scrupulously clean. In the center of the town stood the chapel with a schoolhouse as its wing. Behind the houses were fruitful gardens and orchards. Stretching down to the river were cultivated fields and meadows. The converts had large herds of cattle and hogs, and poultry of every kind. They devoted more time to tilling the ground than to hunting. To the Indians they sold corn, maple sugar, butter, and pork; and to the white settlers they sold dugout canoes made of white pine. The population of Friedenshütten in 1766 had increased to about 150 souls.[6]

Through long and bitter experience, the missionaries learned that in sustained encounter with the white race the Indian would lose out, morally as well as materially. At a missionary conference in 1803 the Moravian missionaries to the Indians pointed out that it was better for Indians to fabricate chairs, baskets, mats, and sieves at home for trade, than to go to work for the white people at harvest time.[7]

Even the briefer contacts with traders created endless problems. In addition to selling liquor to the Indians and cheating them, traders were suspected of trying to turn the Indians against Zeisberger and all whites.[8] The missionaries saw their faith in the Indian's potential tested by the proneness of Christian Indians to succumb to the temptation of drunkenness.[9] Yet occasionally, their faith was signally vindicated, as when Ignatius, an Indian convert, fulfilled a building contract at Gnadenhütten very satisfactorily. Zeisberger's companion of his later journeys, Benjamin Mortimer, an Irish Moravian, observed: "It is a remarkable circumstance, singular perhaps in the history of our times, that a converted heathen, formerly a savage, should build a religious meeting house for the use of a congregation of white Christians."[10] Yet it was not easy to turn nomadic hunters into farmers and herdsmen. The same diarist registered complaints that the Indian Christians at Goshen neglected their cattle, failing to feed and milk the cows regularly.[11]

But the greatest obstacles to the acculturation and economic survival of the Indians were those which the missionaries and the Indians encountered among white men. In the new American nation government support for a program of civilizing the Indians through mission work was uncertain and ambiguous at first.[12] In fact, an Indian reported to the Moravian missionaries that President Thomas Jefferson, at an interview with a group of Indian chiefs, actually advised them against receiving the doctrines which the missionaries taught.[13]

But time and again, the Indian found himself frustrated in his effort to share the prosperity of his white brothers by factors much nearer home. Marauding Indians,[14] wars between the whites, white settlers who refused to trust any Indians, even Christians, were some of the factors that stood between the Indians and a peaceful sharing of the fruits of civilization. Like their red brothers in Massachusetts under John Eliot, the Indians of Zeisberger's Moravian villages became the victims of preying white men. No less than four different places bear the name of Gnadenhütten (not including New Gnadenhütten in Michigan).[15]

The third site of Gnadenhütten, on the Tuscarawas River in Ohio, was the scene of one of the most shameful massacres in American history.[16] The Moravian Indian villages found themselves caught between the upper and the nether millstone in the closing phases of the Revolutionary War. They tried to preserve their neutrality, but both the British and the Americans suspected them of double-dealing. In accordance with both Indian and Christian custom, they extended hospitality to the Indian allies of either side. So many white settlers had lost relatives to Indian war parties that the whole western frontier was thirsting for blood. The war parties vanished into the forests and were hard to trace. The Christian Indians in their settled towns were within easy reach. They became the scapegoats, and the settlers resolved that their "halfway houses" must be destroyed.

From Pittsburgh a group of militia that may have numbered 150 men moved against Gnadenhütten and Salem and gained entrance by the utmost treachery, promising to remove the Indians to a new and safer place. But then they bound the peaceful inhabitants and murdered them two by two in two buildings they wantonly called "slaughter houses." White men, some of whom must have been baptized as Christians, scalped Christian Indians with biblical names who lived in the white men's houses, wore white men's clothing, and used civilized utensils and tools in their homes and their work. Some of the Indians pleaded for their lives in fluent German and English. Yet the pitiless settlers spared not a single one. Six national missionary assistants with their wives were among the murdered. In all, the men of Pittsburgh scalped ninety-six defenseless men, women, and little children.[17] "Some of the finest converts of the

Delaware Nation died that day," mourns a contemporary historian.[18] R. Pierce Beaver renders this judgment: "This evil deed was as senseless and ill-advised as it was wicked, for it drove the whole nation of Delawares into a fury of hate against the Americans. It is one of the most indelible stains on the national honor in the whole long history of treachery and shameful dealing with the Indians."[19]

Unlike the leisure-loving Iberian whites of South America, the more numerous Anglo-Saxon settlers of North America did not feel the urgent need of Indian slaves.[20] And by the time the cotton plantations of the South were expanding in the wake of Eli Whitney's gin, the Indians were regarded as inaccessible, intractable, and not worth the trouble of civilizing. Besides, by then clipper ships were crossing the Atlantic loaded with all the "black ivory" they could hold.

One cannot help wondering what the future of the Indian American and the future of Indian missions might have been if the Moravian experiment had not been choked in blood. The Indian in the New World, like the Jew in the Old, learned the hard way that assimilation to the surrounding culture could not save him from becoming a scapegoat in a period of crisis.

VII

Economic Activities in Labrador

We turn from the smoking carnage of Gnadenhütten to another Moravian mission field, in Labrador. Here, too, violent death attended the first attempt in 1752. John Christian Erhardt, a Herrnhut convert, succeeded in winning the support of three English Moravians for a trading expedition to Labrador, which was to be the vehicle for a mission to the Eskimos. Four Moravian Brethren accompanied Erhardt, though they were to be independent of him as an official mission of the Unitas Fratrum. But they were forced to return to England after the Eskimos murdered Erhardt, together with six companions, on a trading foray.

A Moravian historian finds a main cause of the murders in the fact that amid the Franco-British conflicts of the eighteenth century the Eskimos regarded themselves as friends of the French and therefore as enemies of the British. The right way to approach them was to call out the French word "Ami, ami" (friend) to them, in order to communicate that one had no hostile intentions. Erhardt's people apparently did not know this. At any rate, their ship was flying the English flag.[1]

Zinzendorf had apparently been dubious about the venture from the beginning. The tragic experience at St. Croix had stiffened his opposition to any combination of colonization and mission. However, in Labrador as on St. Croix, inadequate preparation for the venture was the true cause of failure. The one man who could have prevented the tragedy by his skill in communicating with the

Eskimos, Matthias Stach of Greenland, may have been prevented from accompanying the expedition by Zinzendorf himself.[2]

The next serious effort was better prepared. After four exploratory voyages in nineteen years, the carpenter and former Greenland missionary Jens Haven led a group of eleven Brethren to Labrador in 1771. Haven gained the official backing of the governor of Newfoundland, Sir Hugh Palliser, who issued a memorable proclamation:

> Hitherto the Esquimaux have been considered in no other light than as thieves and murderers, but as Mr. Haven has formed the laudable plan, not only of uniting these people with the English nation, but of instructing them in the Christian religion, I require, by virtue of the powers delegated to me, that all men, whomsoever it may concern, lend him all the assistance in their power.[3]

In their work among the Indians in North America, the Moravians had learned the importance of the understanding and support of the authorities. Bitter experience had also taught them that they would need huge reserves of land if the people were to survive in their ancient way of life, and if their mission were to be successful. Therefore, they requested grants of land of not less than 100,000 acres for each mission station, arguing that only in this way could they prevent unscrupulous traders from taking advantage of the Eskimos, as was the prevailing situation in southern Labrador. The authorities, of course, including the favorably inclined Governor Palliser, met this request with extreme suspicion. The Moravians, however, stubbornly held to their demands. Perhaps their rule against personal profit for missionaries helped to persuade the government of their selfless concern for the Eskimos' welfare. At any rate, they succeeded in obtaining grants by Royal Proclamation on the condition that the Moravians "in no respect interrupt or annoy the fisheries carried on upon the said coast of Labrador," which were the chief reason for England's interest in Labrador. The Moravians in turn stipulated that permission to reside on the land grants, for Eskimos and whites alike, would be given only if the residents obeyed the mission rules of good behavior.[4]

An Arctic anthropologist acknowledges that already in Greenland the Brethren had learned "the important lesson that the spiritual life of the Eskimos could not be cultivated without maintaining the economic base upon which their welfare depended."[5] The result was for 170 years an isolated, closed, and protected "Shangri La" for the northern Labrador Eskimos, under Moravian missionaries who had as much authority over nearly all aspects of life as the Roman Catholic padres had on their reductions in Latin America. To the accusation that they were equally paternalistic, the Moravians would reply that their system of land rights and missionary dominance, with all its faults, spelled survival for the Eskimo, as the reductions did for the Indian in Latin America. The Moravians point to southern Labrador where the Eskimos' "freedom" from missionary control resulted in their extermination.[6]

Thanks to his Greenland background Jens Haven was able to communicate freely with the feared Eskimos of Labrador, who spoke a variant of the Greenland tongue.[7] Furthermore, the eleven missionaries had a prefabricated house[8] and plenty of victuals, all transported with them on the *Amity,* a ship acquired by the Labrador Ship Company, a kind of shareholders' trading corporation loosely connected with the mission. The vessel was essential for providing missionaries with transportation and supplies on the lonely coast of Labrador. In 1771 the ship company sent two trading agents to Labrador. But this soon resulted in friction, for the missionaries, too, were forced to trade with the Eskimos for many of their needs, and the traders represented a threatening competition. Furthermore, the missionaries thought that some of the trade goods offered by the agents was harmful to the mission purpose. In 1797 the problem was solved, at least for several generations, by dissolving the Trading Company. From now on, the annual voyage to Labrador and all attendant matters, including trade, were placed under the supervision of the Society for the Furtherance of the Gospel, a Moravian mission auxiliary in London, to which many of the Trading Company leaders belonged.[9] The Society (hereafter referred to as the S.F.G.) had been organized already in 1741.[10] After dissolution in 1750,[11] it was renewed in 1768.[12] Its main activity was to provide hospitality and assistance to Moravian missionaries traveling via England. Its chief intention was "to promote the Gospel and to assist missionaries under British rule in America and other parts of the world."[13] However, from the time of its renewal it saw larger possibilities beyond acting as a farewell and greeting committee. Article 9 of its Constitution even raised the possibility that the Society or one or more of its members might be named trustees of land for a settlement among the heathen, in which case, the article stated, "we promise not to abuse the trust placed on us, and never to lay personal claim to that which has been placed in our name and entrusted to us."[14] Only Moravians could be full members, but others could be honorary or corresponding members.[15] There were also monthly public meetings at which reports from missionaries were read. Even strangers were admitted on the condition that "they behave themselves decently."[16]

Trade offered advantages as well as problems. It proved of value in training the improvident people in habits of thrift and order. When unprincipled white traders tried to exploit the natives, the Moravians gave traders and people alike a demonstration of honest business methods, and by the competition of their example made other traders treat the people more fairly. The opportunity for trade in the Brethren settlements was necessary also to keep the people within reach of their missionaries, away from the temptations introduced by other European traders. It became customary for a large store and warehouse to be built near the church. Often there was also a shed where the native women could take proper care of the blubber.

Meanwhile, for over a century and a half, the *Amity* and a long line of successors, many named *Harmony,* made an annual trip to Labrador. In fact, until the middle of the nineteenth century this ship was the only regular means of communication with the outside world.[17] Not the calendar year but the "ship year" was the working division of time in Labrador.[18] No wonder both the 50th and 100th anniversaries of regular Moravian shipping were observed with services of praise and thanks to God.[19]

The Moravian vessels compiled a remarkable record of safety and reliability.[20] As a matter of fact, it was not until the eighty-fourth voyage in 1853 that the ship failed because of storms to visit all the Labrador stations on its schedule. The effects demonstrate how vital the *Harmony* and the auxiliary society were to the missions. The Brothers in charge of the trade stores had to warehouse for another year the furs and other wares that were ready for shipment. They also missed the new trade goods for the next season. The result was a substantial loss in income.

For years the S.F.G. in London was able to defray all the expenses of the Labrador mission out of the trading profits. Even after the general mission treasury of the church had to step in to defray rising mission costs in a time of increased competition from independent traders and fishermen, the London company continued to be responsible for the trade and the men engaged in business and industry in the Labrador mission.[21]

Rarely in Protestant circles have trade and missions been so long intertwined as in the Moravian missions to Labrador. For this reason it makes an interesting case study. Concern for the people, even more than support of the mission, motivated the Brethren. The Eskimo bartered fish, oil, and furs for weapons, ammunition, cloth, food and necessary tools and utensils. The Society for the Furtherance of the Gospel did not exploit the Eskimo; it did not gain support for the mission by overcharging him. It was content with modest profit margins, which were in turn devoted to the Labrador mission and the welfare of the Eskimos.[22] The mission trade stores deliberately refused to stock luxury items which the bare subsistence economy of the Eskimo could not afford. Frequently the mission stores sold essential goods at cost. The trade stores made it possible to provide for the poor, the sick, and the old in hard winters, and for everyone in poor hunting and fishing years. But this laudable effort led to the unfortunate credit system.

The credit system, which made so much trouble for both sides, had arisen because of the mission's desire to meet the Eskimo's need and to help him through unproductive hunting and fishing seasons. The credit nuisance troubled the Hudson Bay Company and other traders as well, and was based on the uncertainties that naturally attend hunting and fishing. Yet, the missionaries felt that there was a fundamental difference between the mission trade stores and those of other traders, who carried on barter for the sake of their own profit, rather than to help the Eskimo.

From the start the missionary's personal involvement in trade created problems. Perhaps many of these could have been avoided if the S.F.G., as an independent trading association, had from the beginning placed its own agents in charge of the stores and relieved the missionaries of the ambiguities and contradictions into which this activity placed them.

After the missionaries found the difficulties of their double duty behind the pulpit and behind the counter more and more oppressive, the merchant Karl Linder was sent to Labrador in 1864 to make a thorough study of the situation. He recommended the separation of trade from the spiritual aspects of missionary work. Linder himself was placed in charge of all trading operations and certain of the Brethren were to become storekeepers, while the ordained missionaries no longer were to have anything to do with barter. (In actual fact, it took forty years to carry out that resolution completely.)

But it was easier for European than for Eskimo minds to separate religion and business. The Eskimo, who lived in a unified world since time immemorial and had been accustomed for the past century to receive the gospel and his trade goods from one and the same man, simply could not separate the two activities in his own consciousness. He became even more confused when the same man operated in two different ways, depending on whether he was in the church or in the store.

The Eskimos were a trial to the storekeepers. They were quick enough to accept any material help the missionaries had to offer. When hunting and fishing failed and starvation threatened, they demanded relief from the missionary trade stores. But when successful in their trapping and fishing, they often preferred to carry their goods to the traders in the south, where they could buy rum and indulge in vice.[23] In times of plenty the Eskimos had little sense of their obligation to repay their debts.[24]

When the trader at the store operated with new and unaccustomed strictness in enforcing the rules of credit, there was a rising tide of grumbling and rebellion. The missionaries had been rather soft-hearted and careless in advancing credit in the past. Now the rule was laid down that those who had not paid last year's debts should receive no new trade goods from the annual voyage of the *Harmony*. Schulze, who was born in Labrador of Moravian missionary parents, reports: "This ordinance, however, seemed cruel to the Eskimos, and they could not reconcile it with the brotherly love of a missionary who preaches the Gospel."[25] In 1887 at the mission station of Zoar this attitude even led to a public riot. The missionary's life was in danger, for after the fishing catch failed completely, certain of the people planned to plunder the store. A man shot twice into the store where two employees were at work. This occurred in spite of considerable advances to the people from the "poor fund."[26] Similar disturbances took place at Okak in 1873 and at Hebron in 1889.

Yet, the misunderstandings and difficulties were not seen to contravene the basic advantage of having trade and mission proceed at least in close relation with one another. As late as 1904, when the

Moravians founded a new mission station at Ungava Bay, they began
by purchasing the trade store of a Newfoundland firm, for as one
historian declares, "on the basis of long experience it was best, if in
Labrador trade and mission were conducted according to the same
principles."[27]

But in 1906 the separation between trade and mission was further
clarified. Now the S.F.G. became entirely responsible for the trading
operations. It was organizationally distinct and was no longer under
the supervision of the mission board. Now the general mission
treasury became responsible for all regular mission expenses, while
the S.F.G. retained only the administration and financing of trade.
The S.F.G. had its own employees, who no longer preached and
administered the sacraments, but nevertheless worked in the same
spirit as the other missionaries. The S.F.G. remained true to its
original purpose as a missionary trading association, which now as
always devoted itself to the welfare of the Eskimo even more than to
profit.

But the credit nuisance remained. The economic situation of the
Eskimos made it exceedingly difficult to carry on trade without
credit, unless one simply abandoned the Eskimos to their fate in lean
years, as was done at times by some other traders, who felt neither
missionary purpose nor responsibility for the people's welfare. Had
credit been completely refused by the missionaries, this would have
proved completely incomprehensible to the Eskimos, who by nature
help one another most generously. That the mission trade store
aimed also to train them in thrift and in making provision for the
time of need, was simply beyond their understanding.

The credit problem was never solved satisfactorily in a century
and a half. It reached its peak as a result of the inflation of World
War I, during which time the Eskimos made debts at the trade stores,
and then found themselves unable to pay when fur prices returned
to normal after the war. The upshot was that in 1926 the entire
ancient trading operation on the Labrador coast, which had
previously been carried on by the Society for the Furtherance of the
Gospel among the Heathen for the promotion and support of the
Moravian mission, was leased to the well-known Hudson Bay
Company.[28] Also the last mission ship, the fifth *Harmony,* was sold
to the new operators. A recent Moravian history says the mission
agency made this transaction "with a sense of profound relief."[29] It
was not, however, without nostalgia and a sense of loss that the

remarkable 155-year-old tradition was broken off. The nuisance was gone, but so was something of the wholeness of life in the Moravian missions.

On the other hand, the problems of mission administration were eased somewhat. No longer were they dependent on the proceeds of trade, which had for decades suffered from wide variation and steady diminution; now they could work with a fixed annual lease payment. And apparently, the trade stores, which remained the same, were carried on by the new management in good rapport with the missionaries and the mission administration.[30]

However, even the famous Hudson Bay Company found the trade none too profitable. Already in 1942, before the term expired, it gave up the twenty-one-year lease it had signed in 1926. It was taken over by the Department for Northern Labrador Affairs of the government in Newfoundland. From 1943 it provided sufficient food supplies and fishing supplies.[31]

Today the Eskimos, like the settlers and mixed-blood population of Labrador, no longer depend on credit at the trade store. Instead, they rely on many types of social welfare assistance by the Canadian government. Alcohol and tobacco, the latter particularly damaging to the Eskimos because of their proneness to tuberculosis, continue to be social problems. New times and new opportunities have also brought new paternalism, new temptations, and new problems.[32]

VIII

Economic Activities in Surinam

An even older and larger commercial operation is carried on by the Moravians in Surinam (Dutch Guiana), on the northern coast of South America. Zinzendorf's choice of Surinam is easy to explain: the Guianas were the only areas on the South American continent free from the Roman Catholic dominion of Spain and Portugal. The first Moravian messengers arrived in 1735. They sought to bring the gospel to the Indians as well as to the Negro slaves and their descendants. In this period Herrnhut utilized the added potential of new refugee Brethren from Bohemia and Moravia by establishing missionary colonies in Surinam and elsewhere, as for example in Georgia on the Savannah River in 1734. Besides, Zinzendorf's sympathy for the Indians and Negroes in Surinam had been aroused by the tales he had heard already in 1719 when he was in Holland.[1]

The first Moravian missionaries addressed themselves to the Arawak Indians, who were then still numerous. But the missionary colonists on their remote plantations needed someone in the chief city to forward supplies. Two Brethren, Dehne and Ralfs, were sent to open the agency in 1754. Whatever time was left after expediting supplies to the missionaries in the hinterland was to be spent earning their own living as tailors. If their tailor shop produced more than enough for their own living, the balance was to help support the Indian mission. Good work punctually delivered soon won for them more orders than they could fill. Their well-to-do customers wanted clothes for themselves plus liveries for their man-servants and uniforms for their household help—naturally all slaves, who fancied these fine feathers. Dehne and Ralfs had to employ outside help to satisfy their customers, some of whom belonged to the highest circles. The only people they could hire were slaves, whom they rented from their masters. Later Ralfs bought two slaves, which was cheaper in the long run than renting them from their masters. It must have scandalized some Brothers, but the slaves were better off with Brethren as masters.[2]

Sitting on a tailor's bench together it was easy to converse about the gospel. The missionaries gradually gained influence with these slaves and through them got in touch with other slaves in the town. The rented tailor's shop grew and enabled them to buy their own plot of land. They added a bakery and a watchmaker's business. More and more Negroes came in contact with them. The number of their employees grew and so did their influence over them, for they gave them not only work but a new way of life. The white population became convinced that this influence was good and changed their attitude toward the mission. The first Negro, a freedman, was baptized in 1776, and several slaves followed his example in 1778. In the same year the Brethren built a little chapel for their converts. Not only black faces appeared at the services, but every now and then white faces also. Even the governor, who had become persuaded that a blessing rested on these Moravian tailors, bakers, and watchmakers, showed them much kindness and supported their work.[3] While, ironically, the mission carried on by the more conventional missionaries dwindled, the mission of the tailors, the bakers, and the watchmakers to the Negroes of Paramaribo blossomed so that by 1926 with thirteen thousand members worshipping in seven church buildings it was the largest Moravian congregation in the world.[4]

The original stimulus to this outright commercial activity had apparently come not from the field but from headquarters in Germany. The men of Herrnhut encouraged the Brethren in Surinam to establish plantations, start cattle raising, and open a shoemaker's shop. After a tailor shop opened in the neighboring British colony of Berbice, it branched out into selling goods shipped by the Brethren in Europe. Out of a chest of striped linen and some miscellaneous manufactured articles shipped out to Paramaribo in 1758, a whole department store plus other activities developed by 1900. It is interesting to trace the beginnings of that enterprise.

It all began at a meeting of the *Heidendiakonie,* a kind of mission board meeting in Herrnhut on April 23, 1758. The *Heidendiakonie* had been organized in 1754 especially for the financial administration of the mission activities. Some thirty brothers and sisters were being sent out to Surinam, including a shoemaker for the shop at Berbice, a tailor to help fill mounting orders in Paramaribo, a weaver who was also a mason and a hunter, a baker and musician. The minutes drip with the blood, sweat, and tears of a committee cudgelling its brains to find the travel costs for such a party of missionary colonists leaving the very next day.[5] A significant note on the margin of the minutes, evidently added later, reads: "At the departure of the Brethren . . . the great lack of travel funds and the fact that much money had already been advanced brought up the idea of sending striped linen [to Surinam] . . . out of which the Brethren Commercial Society soon developed."[6]

In the beginning is the idea. Whose was the fertile mind that planted a department store with the seed of a small chest of striped linen? Odds are that it was Jonas Paul Weiss, a member of the *Heidendiakonie.* Weiss had been a Nürnberg merchant at one time, and had made attempts to start textile manufacturing in Herrnhut as early as 1739.[7] Sometime between the day of the board meeting and the end of April he wrote a long letter to the Brethren in Surinam containing some hard pioneer thinking on economic activities in missions.

In Surinam, the Brethren were able to avoid one of the problems they had encountered in Labrador. In the north the trade goods had simply been dumped on the preaching missionary, for whom it was often a necessary evil. But in the tropics the Brethren from the beginning sent out special artisans and business people. This happened because of the sound thinking of the people already on the field. One of them responded to the plan by observing that he had no objection to commerce, but that a brother with a good head for business would have to be sent out expressly for the purpose. He added:

> The people here are very bad and expert in all evil. A man would have to be very wise and experienced, otherwise he could be badly cheated. Among the brothers here now there is no one with either the head or the heart for this.[8]

Together with their commerce and crafts, the Moravian "laymen"

also witnessed to their faith. But this extra was not a necessary evil
to them. As Christian laymen they considered it perfectly natural
and did it with joy. All of which goes to show that it is usually easier
for a businessman to witness than for a preacher to conduct a
business on the side.

In a significant letter, Weiss reveals both his business brain and his
missionary heart. He cannot understand why the Brethren craftsmen
in Paramaribo could not also sell some merchandise on the side. He
takes a daring swing at the mediaeval notion that commerce as
distinguished from craft is in itself dishonorable. He could see no
essential difference between selling someone a custom-made suit and
selling him a piece of linen. One was as honorable, brotherly, and
Christian as the other. And the temptation to greed, cunning, fraud,
and exploitation could arise as easily in making a suit as in selling a
piece of goods. The hard-pressed mission board member could see no
reason why their colony of apostles should deprive itself of the
advantages of honest commerce. He broke the news that it had been
decided to make a small beginning and send out one small chest of
striped linen and other merchandise for sale.[9] Nor could Weiss agree
with the popular notion that agriculture was holier than commerce:

> A man sells his corn, wood, beer, brandy, etc., makes a profit
> and regards it as the blessing of God. But he is afraid that he
> plunges into sin, if he sells some goods that are sent out to him
> at whatever price obtains in that country for such goods and
> makes a profit.

Weiss argued that voluntary contributions were inadequate for the
size of the missionary task. He contended that the apostolate to the
heathen could best become a permanent and total blessing, if it were
supported by a colony or settlement. Such missionary colonies
would need business enterprises. He asks, "Did the fact that there
was a profit-making shoemaker's shop at Pilgerhuth stop the Gospel
from being preached to the heathen?" As a man of experience, Weiss
declared that business enterprises would produce more profit than
agriculture or crafts, though the latter enjoyed theological favor. It
was not opportunism but a sense of stewardship that moved him to
promote with joy the experiment of sending a small chest of striped
linen for sale in Surinam. "When such a good opportunity presents
itself as we have, we are making a mistake if we fail to use it or
neglect it because of onesided ideas." In business, Weiss saw as many
opportunities for Christian witness as for profit:

It takes as much grace to act graciously as a child of God in buying and selling as for many other acts which pass for spiritual and are held in high regard. I deem a brother as worthy of all honor and love, who does not lose this viewpoint, but holds fast to the joy of serving not his cause but that of the Savior and his neighbor.

Martin Luther would have applauded the distinction Weiss sought to preserve between the vocations of the various Brethren. He was not suggesting that "the man who in the forenoon sells a piece of merchandise stand up and preach in the afternoon." He saw no reason why these could not be kept separate. But he did insist that the man who leads a hymn-sing skillfully or the man who preaches well is no more important than the man who can get along well in business with the people of the community. "Friendly, firm, loving and ready to serve . . . [such a businessman] persuades the people that life must really be different among the Brethren, because he is such a good man and yet knows how to get along so well and so properly with the people." Weiss recognized that demonstration is as important as proclamation in the Christian world mission. He knew that Christian businessmen practicing their "faith active in love" in the daily affairs of the market place rather than hidden away in a monastery would be powerful audiovisual aids in Christian missions.[10]

Weiss argues his case so insistently that one may easily suspect that he has an axe to grind, as indeed he does. But what was his axe? As a member of the Herrnhut Directorium he was painfully aware of the situation confronting the board: 1) There was no lack of Moravian refugees willing and ready to go out as missionaries. 2) The giving capacity of the Moravians and their circle of friendly supporters had been taxed to the utmost already. 3) And yet the directors lacked funds for the most essential needs of a missionary party leaving the very next day. Weiss was aware of the great need abroad for the gospel. With the fields white unto the harvest and plenty of laborers ready to go, Weiss was unwilling to cut the missionary enterprise back to the level of cash-giving capacity. If the workers were on hand, his preferred solution was finding additional financial resources, even if this meant violating ancient Moravian prejudices against trade. Because of these old taboos, Weiss knew he had to present basic and detailed arguments if he wished to revolutionize the attitudes of Moravian artisan missionaries toward commerce.

Meanwhile the growing business of Abraham Dürninger at Herrnhut had sent larger shipments of linen to Cadiz, Bayonne, Livorno, Basel, Bern, and Utrecht in 1753; in 1754 Harlem and New York were added; in 1755, Bilbao and Lisbon. By 1767 even the Royal Prussian Trading Company would feel the competition of Dürninger's linen. No doubt, Dürninger's middle-man role as exporter for the weavers of the Oberlausitz had occasioned discussion and debate in Herrnhut. And Weiss was, no doubt, now applying to the needs of Surinam the new arguments that had been marshalled to justify Dürninger's commercial activities. Weiss saw no reason why the Surinam mission and the Directorium should not avail themselves of the opportunity to develop financial resources for the Surinam mission that lay ready to hand in Dürninger's linen wares.

The Moravians were fortunate in Jonas Paul Weiss. Rarely have Protestant mission boards in these past two centuries exhibited the kind of bold and basic thinking that characterized this man, whose only concern was the welfare of the mission. Weiss did not subordinate his principles to seeking profit at any price. In the same letter, he warned the Brethren in Surinam against buying Negro slaves for their plantations. His entire letter is undogmatic, and he invites the missionaries to take out of it only what seems good to them.

The Brethren in Surinam thought so well of Weiss's ideas that ultimately in 1768 a business firm was organized under the name C. Kersten & Co.,[11] which proved to be for generations the financial backbone of the Moravian mission to Surinam. (The name is rich in symbolism. Literally translated, Christoph Kersten & Co. means "Christ-bearer Christian & Co.," truly a fitting name for a missionary and a company that helped lay the foundation for Christianizing the Guianas, especially when one recalls that the "& Co." can mean only the Unity of the Brethren, to this day the sole stockholder. The man on the street called it "C.K.C.")[12] It would take too much space to describe the enterprise in detail. It must suffice to list some of the chief activities in which it engaged. The department store sold manufactured goods, groceries, and hardware. There was a book store, a large bakery, and a watch shop. The firm had branches in various towns. It owned plantations, whose income fluctuated with business conditions, the weather, and the inroads of plant diseases. It also operated a sizeable building business, which erected structures needed by the mission but also took outside contracts for profit.[13]

By entering into business, the Moravians also entered into the economic structures of society, including the institution of slavery. As pragmatic liberals, the Moravians carried on mission and service to humanity within the limits of the possible. Contrary to Weiss's advice, C. Kersten & Co. did purchase slaves. By 1800, it owned 40. Some of them were purchased out of pure compassion, as when a communicant member of the church was being sold at auction.[14] However, such steps identified the Brethren with the "establishment."[15] The Moravians became slaveholders also in St. Thomas and Jamaica, where they owned plantations. These actions relieved much of the early mistrust of the Moravians among the "plantocracy" and governing circles in Dutch-held Surinam.[16]

In neighboring Berbice, ruled by the British, the Brethren, however, refused on principle to own slaves.[17] Nor was there always agreement in Surinam. One blow for the abolition of slavery was struck by Nils Otto Tank. The brilliant son of a proud Norwegian family, Tank had been considered as a possible successor to the Norwegian throne until his conversion to the Moravian Church and his marriage to a Moravian girl. Consecrated a bishop, he came to Surinam where he served as chairman of the mission and head of C. Kersten & Co. While in Europe, Tank dropped a bombshell by publishing a brochure in the revolutionary year 1848 "To the Gentlemen Owners and Administrators of Plantations in the Colony Surinam." After that, he could not return to Surinam.[18]

Other attempts to help the slaves were made by the Surinam congregation, which had a special fund for the purchase of freedom for slaves amounting to almost 9,000 guilders in 1850, as well as a Marriage Promotion Fund.[19]

When it came to direct mission work, the Moravians did not hesitate to go their own way. The Reformed Church Council demanded that Negroes learn to read Dutch before they could be baptized. Moravians took them as they were.[20] From 1832 manumitted slaves had to give proof of enrollment in a church.[21] This aided Moravian mission efforts. By 1860 Moravians were active on nearly all the plantations still in operation, about 150.[22]

In 1863, by coincidence the same year as in the United States, emancipation was proclaimed. It changed the status of the slave

from that of a legal object to that of a legal subject.[23] It was
accomplished without civil strife. Emancipation day, July 1, 1863,
was observed with solemn church services, none better attended than
those of the Moravians who had prepared the slaves for this day.[24]
It is ironic to reflect that in a slave society, the Christian Church had
achieved better integration than is generally true in the United States
of the 1960's. All Christian congregations of Surinam had black
members by 1863. And no one had contributed more to this
koinonia than the Moravians, who worked within the social system,
but quietly undermined it by initiating slaves into the Unity of the
Brethren. Within that Unity both slaves and freemen served one
Master through both business and mission.

For a long time the relation between business and mission was
most intimate. At the General Synod of 1848, ninety years after
Weiss's chest of striped linen, it was acknowledged that the business
enterprises were essential to the support of the rapidly expanding
mission work in Surinam. By 1869, a century after the founding of
C. Kersten & Co., the idea of separating the mission from a business
that had been signally blessed was seriously raised but quickly
rejected as inadvisable.

Until the middle of the 1880's the mission in Surinam needed no
subsidy from the general mission treasury. The following comparative tables from 1888 to 1897 are revealing:

Surinam Mission Finances[25]

	Total Expense	Provincial Income	Subsidy
1888	235,591.26	201,910.58	33,680.68
1897	296,897.81	197,431.81	99,466.00

Sources of Provincial Income

	1888	1897
General contributions	14,904.75	17,137.30
Commerce, crafts, agriculture	86,520.90	60,322.00
Government grants, interests and special income	98,029.18	113,328.11
Voluntary offerings	2,455.75	6,644.40
Total marks	201,910.58	197,431.81

Commercial income was falling. And energetic efforts to increase indigenous church offerings could not make up for it. Though there was a large percentage increase in indigenous church offerings, serious financial problems would have resulted without increased revenue from government grants, interest, and special income. Had the group during more than a century become too dependent on such income? Was the effort to promote individual and congregational stewardship initiated too late? We recognize, of course, that the giving power of the people, mostly former slaves, was low. Furthermore, one should be careful in drawing unfavorable comparisons with indigenous efforts elsewhere, for in few other places was there also an attempt to recoup missionaries' salaries through indigenous income.[26]

But by the turn of the century a process began which in 1928 culminated in an organizational separation between mission and business. Significantly, the reasons which led to this step were precisely the opposite from those which had prompted the same result in Labrador. In the north it was the mission which suffered by having to carry on trade. In the tropics it was the business which suffered and was inhibited by its too intimate connection with the mission. The report of the mission board to the General Synod of 1909 declared that while the mission work had been going forward, the business was standing still, if not retrogressing. A complete reorganization of the enterprise was regarded as essential if the goal of self-support for the missionary province was to be achieved. This was seen as unthinkable unless the business profits could be increased. Such increase could be expected only if the enterprises were taken out of their close connection with the mission and were conducted in the future by businessmen from a business viewpoint.

During World War I the process of separation was arrested because the mission for a number of years had to rely on the business for its total support.[27] However, the business was so weakened as a result of giving so many budgetary transfusions to the mission during World War I that the great firm of C. Kersten and Company, oldest and largest German firm in the colony, almost died. The final separation of the business and the Surinam province was facilitated when the Moravian mission in Surinam was transferred from German direction to the Dutch Moravians of the Zeist Mission Society in 1928, while C. Kersten & Co. was placed under the direct supervision of a foundation, *Die Missionsanstalt der*

Evangelischen Brüder-Unität (The Mission Institute of the Moravian Church) at Herrnhut.

Today C. Kersten & Co. is by far the largest trading company in Surinam, employing over 1,350 people. Its enterprises in the Netherlands Antilles provide work for 200 additional people, and other branches have been opened in Amsterdam, New York, and Hamburg. Though wages once were low,[28] the company has paid a bonus out of profits to its personnel ever since 1910.[29] Employees also enjoyed a substantial discount on their own purchases. Outstanding among twentieth-century heads of the firm was Siegfried Beck, who managed it from 1908 to 1927. He is described as having had more social sensibility than mercantile spirit.[30] He stopped the sale of alcohol in 1910.[31] The company long maintained a fire department for the entire community.[32] Today it offers its employees the services of a social worker as well as a doctor.[33] In addition to trade, C. Kersten & Co. now stresses manufacturing and services. These diversified current enterprises include a large department store, hotel, lunchroom, parking garage, insurance department, wholesale pharmaceutical department, bakery, wholesale drapery goods department, agricultural center, beer distributorship, produce and warehouse department, sugar department, bicycle and motorbike department, a taxi company, automobile dealership with repair facilities, an agency for heavy tractors and earth-moving machinery, the manufacture of building supplies, land and water transport, a bottling works for soft drinks, a mattress factory, a shoe factory, and a number of plantations. And under the name "Colon" a modern shopping center is operated on the island of Curacao.[34] C. Kersten & Co.'s yearly contribution to the church runs in the lower six figures of Surinam guilders (a Surinam guilder = 53 cents US).[35] Both the financial help of C. Kersten & Co. and the Christian example of its workers have made a valuable contribution to Moravian missions in Surinam and elsewhere through two centuries. Moravian historians have repeatedly expressed gratitude to the company for its accomplishments during the past two centuries. They have praised it as a firm guided by solid Christian principles. It plays an essential role of far-reaching influence in the business life of Surinam, thereby also providing moral support for the church's work.[36]

This mission firm exerted a beneficent influence on wide circles in the city of Paramaribo through its enlightened and effective promotion of social welfare,[37] especially on behalf of its own large staff of employees numbering hundreds. It provided for an old-age pension and medical insurance when these ideas were still relatively untried in the United States; it erected large homes for apprentices; it conducted in-service training courses and assisted workers in the purchase of their own homes.[38]

In the twentieth century C. Kersten & Co. has successfully met some of its severest tests. In the first decade, unhealthy expansion had been accompanied by a careless extension of credit. This violated a Moravian principle dating back to the early days of the Surinam enterprise. Marcus Ralfs, one of the first two tailors who laid the foundation for C. Kersten & Co., had proved to be a poor bookkeeper and an even worse bill collector.[39] The Mission Board in Europe thereafter forbade credit.[40] As a result of costly experience in the twentieth century, the company soon returned to its long-standing "No Credit" policy. During World War I its affiliation with the international Unitas Fratrum helped the company to get its name off the black list which the Allies drew up for all German companies. Yet the firm suffered because its trade with the Netherlands all but ceased. Even a very recent American Moravian history, which, in keeping with the view of many American Moravians, has little sympathy for the church's involvement in business, pays C. Kersten & Co. this tribute: "During the early 1920's the business had come to the financial aid of the Surinam Province, which could not otherwise have survived in the postwar period."[41] The worldwide depression of the 1930's hit a colonial backwater like Surinam especially hard. But through retrenchment and careful management "Kersten," as it is now popularly called, weathered the storm. With the outbreak of World War II the company lost much of its managerial personnel. Fourteen department heads with other key leaders were interned as enemy aliens. They were German citizens, and almost all of them had contributed to the Nazi Party. After this management crisis, top leadership for the first time came into Dutch hands.[42] The company's capacity for survival was due to many factors, among them its broad diversification, its adaptability, and the excellent business relations it had cultivated over the years.[43]

During the Nazi occupation of Holland in World War II, C. Kersten & Co. was expropriated by the government of Surinam as "enemy property." This critical situation touched off a reorganization.

But before we examine this, we must briefly sketch the

organizational framework to 1941. Originally, C. Kersten & Co. had been directly controlled by the Moravian Church through normal mission board channels. But when the realization dawned that organizational distinction would be helpful to both mission and business, the trading enterprises of the Unity were made the legal property of a corporate body established in 1894 at Herrnhut under the name of the "Mission Institute of the Evangelical Unity of the Brethren." This functioned as a holding company of the various businesses. Besides C. Kersten & Co., it also controlled the firm of "Casa Alemana" in Nicaragua; the expanded *Süd-Afrika West Handel,* with eight branch stores; two stores in Southeast Africa; and a Nyasaland company known as *Handlung der Missionsanstalt der Evangelischen Brüder-Unität.* All these trading businesses served the cause of mission self-support and the needs of the local population.[44] As a result of its expropriation in World War II, C. Kersten and Co. was separated from the Herrnhut holding company in 1941 and became a limited liability company with its seat in Paramaribo. The Moravian Church ultimately transferred the office of the Mission Institute from Herrnhut to the Netherlands, organizing it as a Dutch corporation, and in 1950 it acquired the entire stock of C. Kersten & Co., holding it for the whole Unity. Thus, after a lapse of nine years "Kersten" was returned to its rightful owner.[45]

The foundation holding the stock is *Zendingstichting der Evangelischen Broederuniteit,* incorporated at Zeist, Holland, in 1951. The *Zendingstichting,* or Mission Institute, is a nonprofit corporation created by the General Synod of the Moravian Church for the financial support of the foreign mission work of the Moravian Church in general, as distinct from the work carried on by any Provincial Mission Board. The charter, based on the General Synod of 1948, describes as the object of the *Zendingstichting* the support and furtherance of the mission work of the Moravian Church, in particular by collecting and furnishing funds for the support of Christian congregations among the heathen, for the vocational training, salaries, and pensions of the missionaries, for the education of their children and provision of their widows, and for the administration of property collected for mission work. The charter goes on to say that the Institute obtains its funds from voluntary contributions by members and friends of the Moravian Church as well as "from the earnings of its commercial and industrial undertakings, founded in several mission fields."[46] The board of directors of the Mission Institute consists of representatives of the Moravian Church in the U.S.A. and Europe.

Under Jozias de Kraker, a non-Moravian, as general manager, C. Kersten prospers today and serves its historic missionary objectives. The company is committed to the principle that mission and business are to be distinguished but not separated from each other. Having its own distinct organization helped the business support the mission better.[47] The company finds its reason for existence in supporting the mission,[48] not only by the profits it earns, but by the manner in which it earns them.[49]

The business helps the mission to live in symbiosis with the whole community. It helps the leaven achieve a mix with the loaf instead of segregating it.[50] The business touches people of every stratum of life in Surinam from the most obscure to the most prominent. Archibald Currie, a member of Kersten's Board of Directors, became Governor of Surinam, the first local citizen to hold the highest office in the land.[51] The symbiotic function of leavening runs the inevitable risk of conforming to the world instead of transforming it. Kersten took that risk, generally with open eyes. Dedication to mission preserved the missionary merchants from going too far in adapting to society.

Every employee of C. Kersten & Co., especially expatriates, clearly understood the missionary purpose of the firm. Since 1912 all employees were informed that immediate dismissal would be the penalty for conduct that impaired or hindered the missionary work of the Evangelical Unity of the Brethren. Expatriate employees would in that case have to pay their own return passage. An Employee Regulation of 1915 declares:

> The missionary companies must support and promote the missionary work. Therefore the companies can only engage employees of clearly Christian disposition, who seek their appointment not only for the money or superficial advantages involved, but through personal devotion cooperate in the Christian moral edification of the local population, and thus subject themselves in every respect to Christian discipline and custom, rejecting everything that can cause scandal or unfavorably influence the missionary work.[52]

Christian dedication was furthered by the 7 a.m. Moravian devotions with which C. Kersten & Co. formerly began the working day.[53] In 1912 the company abandoned the egalitarian missionary salary scale and began paying its managerial personnel according to responsibility and achievement.[54] However, this did not lead to a loss in missionary purpose.

Missionary dedication still rings clearly in Helman's thoughtful history published at the bicentennial. Unlike the Basel Mission Trading Co., which we shall consider in Part II, C. Kersten & Co. did not allow world war and the temporary alienation of its property to lead to a permanent separation between mission and business. There is a marked contrast here between Helman and Gustav Wanner, the historian of the Basel Company. For Wanner the missionary purpose and framework of the business is largely history; for Helman it is a vital present reality. Not only is Kersten far older than the Basel Mission Trading Co., but it has held to its missionary dedication far longer and far more wholeheartedly. It is deeply persuaded of at least three reasons for continuing its close association with the mission: 1) the apostolic example of Paul, the tent-making missionary; 2) the entry into and identification with the community provided by economic activities, which prevent the mission from remaining an isolated, encapsuled ghetto; 3) two hundred years of historic fact, which it can successfully place into the balance against any merely theoretical arguments.[55]

As a remarkable contemporary example of Pauline tent-making in missions, Kersten deserves to be far better known than it is. It illustrates the need for a new missionary encounter between the church of Jesus Christ and the business community. The missionary often leads an unreal existence as a kind of ecclesiastical "remittance man" not related to the real life of the society around him. For the sake of its own highest goals, the mission needs to enter the warp and woof of society's fabric. How can it redeem society without entering into it? How else can it get next to people and witness to them?

Kersten's able bicentennial historian sees a new ecumenical encounter shaping up. He goes back to the root meaning of *oikoumene* as "the whole inhabited world." Here an acute and fateful confrontation is in process between the rich and the poor. He sees Kersten as an example of a practical, purposeful way to bridge the gulf between them and to help the poor to help themselves in such a way that they retain their own most precious possession, their human dignity.[56] In this sense, he sees Kersten as a genuine business "concern," in the most practical Christian sense of that word.[57]

Helman holds up C. Kersten & Co. as one way in which Christians on God's mission can "company" together—that is, in the root meaning of the word, to share the same pantry, the same bread, as they form one community of bread and work. The "company" of the Lord's Table becomes an added dimension for the Moravians in their missionary community of bread and work. For the "& Co." in C. Kersten & Co. is nothing else but the worldwide Unity of the Brethren.[58]

IX

Economic Activities in Africa

Because they considered the whole congregation a missionary task force, Moravian missionaries nearly everywhere considered it natural to enter into agricultural and commercial work. Georg Schmidt, a simple, faithful Christian who had spent six years in prison for his faith in Bohemia,[1] reached Capetown alone[2] in 1737. In Bavianskloof, near Capetown, he found a willing response from the Hottentots, who were kept in hard bondage by the Boer farmers. The white colonists thought it odd enough that anyone should preach to these creatures or "shepsels" as they called them. But when the Moravian missionary dared to baptize some of them in 1742, the enmity of the Boers forced him to give up his work. The colonists may have feared that the baptism of slaves would mean manumission. But while this may have been the basic economic factor at work among them, the overt attack, as led by the Reformed clergy in a complaint to Amsterdam, made the following charges: 1) Schmidt was not Reformed but belonged to the Herrnhut sect; 2) his ordination was invalid because performed by letter rather than by the laying on of hands; 3) his *manner* of baptizing was unchurchly because he had baptized in a river and without the presence of a congregation. These charges brought about the end of Schmidt's efforts. However, almost half a century later, in 1792, three Moravian missionaries came to Capetown, and Georg Schmidt's mission was resurrected on the very same site. They found a pear tree Schmidt had planted—and Magdalena, eighty years old and blind, one of seven converts whom he had baptized. They changed the name of Bavianskloof (Baboons' Glen) to "Genadendal"—Valley of Grace—which by 1926 came to be a Christian town of over three thousand.[3]

In addition to their evangelistic efforts, the missionaries at the Cape from the beginning fostered trade, industry, and agriculture—the last with the help of irrigation. They not only wanted to help the people but they wished to relieve the Brethren at home as much as possible in the matter of financial support. Trained businessmen developed business enterprises which in good years showed a considerable profit in support of the mission.[4] Already in 1882 one historian could report that in Genadendal there were not only chapels and training schools but also smithies and shops for carpenters, wheelwrights, and the manufacture of coarse cutlery.[5]

The Moravian industries and farms brought support to the mission and self-respect to the people. Their example had a most pervasive influence, so that people who were proverbial for idleness, inefficiency, and contempt of labor came to work industriously in agriculture and various mechanical arts. An early monument to Hottentot skill was a big bridge over the Sonderend. When the Sonderend was in flood stage, a farmer who had just passed over it met a Hottentot standing by. He began, as usual, to rail at the poor man, and at the laziness of the Hottentots of Genadendal. The Hottentot, pointing to the bridge, replied: "Baas, I do not choose to answer; let that bridge speak for us. If baas had built it for me, and I could without trouble walk and ride over it, I should not venture to complain of baas's laziness. For I should think it required more diligence and labor to build a bridge than to ride over it."[6]

Today, the old mission shops in South Africa's Western Cape Province are no longer directly operated by the missionaries themselves. In 1934, the last two mission shops still run by a station missionary were leased to other people. At present, all mission shops are leased to both nonwhites and white tenants, "but they are Moravians and not working against the spirit of the Church."[7] The fact that they are accountable to a committee composed of missionaries ensures such a result. In 1963, the property of these mission shops was handed over to the *Morawiese Broederkerk in die Westelike Kaapprovinsie* (most of the members of that church being nonwhite). The income from the rents is used—as it was when the shops were mission-owned—for the pensions of former missionaries of that church.[8]

In the Eastern Cape Province and Transkei, where the work began in 1828, the Moravian Church of South Africa East, whose membership consists mostly of Bantus, is more or less self-supporting aside from missionary salaries and expenses, which are paid by the Moravian Mission Account of South Africa. The source of that account, in addition to overseas contributions, is income from one rented shop and a sheep ranch. "Both are run by Europeans who are not missionaries, but of course not against the spirit of the Mission."[9]

In the Tanganyika Southern Highlands Region, where Moravian work began in 1891, the mission itself grew coffee and later tea on a plantation at Kyimbila, near Tukuyu, for about a decade until World War II. Besides an industrial school it also operated a carpentry shop less for the purpose of earning money than to help the people. As the mission owned more land than it could use, it sold some land to a plantation company for shares in the company. "These shares were sold in 1963, the money received being a much needed reserve for the Moravian Church in Southern Tanganyika."[10]

The Moravian missionaries at the Cape served the people not only in ecclesiastical and economic functions but also in a political way. Here we see in a Protestant setting much the same arrangement as the Jesuits followed in the Paraguay reductions:

> The old stations were so-called "Grant stations" and the law which made them such recognized the mission as proprietor of the land, but made it responsible not only for the religious activities of the church, but also for the civil administration of the community life in all respects.[11]

Like the Paraguay reductions, the grant stations of South Africa were created at the urging of the government. First the Dutch, and later the English authorities,[12] requested the missions to assume responsibility for them in order to provide a refuge for the Hottentots, who call themselves *Koi-koin* or *Khoikhoi,* which means "men of men." The Hottentots were the first African people the Dutch encountered in South Africa. They were soon subjugated. And while in 1828 they were released from serfdom, they had by this time been largely detribalized. They had even lost their culture and language, and were using the Afrikaans language of the Dutch, whom they served as menial workers and slaves. Without rights or protection, they were at the mercy of masters who were often cruel. "They were like leaves torn from the tree by the storm and now being blown aimlessly back and forth on the ground," says a Moravian missionary.[13] The missionaries were unable to do effective work among the scattered people without settling them at a fixed habitation.[14] Thus the grant of a large tract of land on which the Hottentots could find security under the administration of the missionaries originally served not only the best interests of the Hottentots but of the missionary work as well. Not only the Moravians, but virtually all larger missions in South Africa had grant stations, among them the Rhenish,[15] Anglican, and Wesleyan missions and the London Missionary Society.

But while the "grant stations" were perhaps the only possible answer to the problem in the beginning, when missionaries were the only group that could be counted on by the government to care about the oppressed and neglected Hottentots, as time went on many tensions, problems, and basic errors in the construction of the grant station system revealed themselves. These caused continual frustration for the missionaries. To be at one and the same time both policeman[16] and preacher of the gospel involved the missionary in endless contradictions.[17] As custodian of law and order the missionary even had to go to court against his people.[18]

Two other problems arose as time went on. The first was occasioned by the generally improved treatment of Africans in the Cape region. Now it was possible for an industrious Hottentot elsewhere to acquire land and property. But the grant stations were bound by antiquated laws of communal ownership.[19] In addition, it was highly uncertain whether the grant station land belonged to the respective mission or to the African community that lived on it. This legal vagueness created endless controversy. The Moravian missionaries themselves took the initiative in persuading the government to settle the issue.[20] Finally, in 1909 the Cape parliament passed the *Mission Land Bill,* or *Mission Stations Act,* which provided for a division in the land of each former grant station. One part was to be the uncontested property of the respective mission society, while the rest of the land belonged to the African community, which administered it through a council, thus relieving the missionary of prime responsibility for communal administration.[21] Now it was up to majority decision in the community whether to retain communal ownership or to divide the land into individual properties. In this way, the Moravians led the way in an economic and political adjustment to a changed situation.

X

Balance Sheet on Moravian
Economic Activities for Missions

In the affluent society of the United States, the Moravian Church has moved far away from the pre-Revolutionary "General Economy" at Bethlehem, Pennsylvania. The church follows the usual American pattern of support by gifts from members or by income from invested funds. Apparently, few American Moravians sympathize with efforts to support missions by commercial enterprises.[1] This peculiar American viewpoint must create certain tensions within the worldwide Unity.

Significantly, European Moravians give business generous space and recognition in their basic constitution and bylaws.[2] This constitution regards the working day as just as holy as Sunday; work is never meaningless, because Jesus works for us. Inherited church enterprises are not a problem, but a reason for thanking God. In such economic activities European Moravians see the chance to serve God and build up his church. Administrators and employees are expected to exhibit faithfulness, a fraternal Christian spirit, and genuine social concern. The mature experience of the Moravian reflects itself in a Christian willingness to accept both "success and failures, which characterize business life." Reverses should be seen as admonitions to humility and trust in God.[3]

In Europe Moravians articulate a comprehensive concept of Christian stewardship. They carefully point out that church enterprises are a supplement to, not a substitute for, personal

71

thank offerings. They are a trust from God, an aid toward fulfilling the tasks of the church, and a source of employment and community life for brothers and sisters.[4]

Within the Unity of the Brethren, the principle prevailed that to be a Moravian and to further missions are identical.[5] While a number of mission societies were organized to aid Moravian missions, these were true auxiliary societies and not surrogates relieving the church of its primary responsibility.[6]

The Moravian principle of the total church as a mission to the world also preserved this church from the one-sided clericalism that overtook many other Protestant missions. The Moravians created an essential and honored role for the artisan and especially the businessman in its worldwide mission. The latter was allowed to do more than keep the accounts of mission expenses. He was given free scope for what a businessman ultimately has to do if he wants to stay in business—make a profit.

In the early years Moravian missionaries frequently worked their passage: "Travel now—pay later" was a time-honored Moravian procedure. The artisan would pay for his trip out of his earnings upon arrival. Once on the field, he was expected to live with other Moravian missionaries in a common household with a community of goods[7] that would have passed muster in the first church at Jerusalem or in a California hippie colony.

Field expenses were for more than a century covered by indigenous income. As late as 1857, the General Synod of the worldwide Moravian Church stated that the missions in Surinam, South Africa, and Labrador were supported entirely from local sources. It is regrettable that this commendable practice could not be continued into the modern nationalistic era, which cries out for it. Moravian authorities vacillated on the question of using Mission Board monies to finance commercial enterprises. In 1899 the General Synod voiced no objection; in 1909 and again in 1914 it asked the Board to take mission monies out of the enterprises.

In evaluating the Moravian tent-making enterprises it would be a mistake to focus entirely on the fact that they are today organizationally distinct from the mission and to forget the many valuable contributions they made over more than two centuries. While faith and love for the Savior were the fuel, these business enterprises were the rockets that hoisted pioneer Moravian satellites into the missionary heavens in an age when other Protestants were doing next to nothing.

Economic activities were a means of sharing a better physical and material life with the people of mission lands. Moravians did their best to ease the transition of less advanced people into the crafts and industries of a technologically more progressive culture. The range of economic activities is impressive. From a combination saw- and flour mill at Gnadenhütten,[8] as the economic mainstay of this Lehigh River Moravian Indian Village, to reindeer herding in Alaska,[9] the Brethren ran the gamut.

To this day productive enterprises founded by the Moravians, though no longer directly united with the missions, are apparently on good fraternal terms with the latter under the overall supervision of the Unitas Fratrum. This provided an organizational unity within which diverse thrusts could be contained and reconciled. In part, this may explain why the Moravians have been able to maintain their connection with the large firm of C. Kersten & Co. for two centuries. In all historic vicissitudes, the church organization of the Moravians generally stood them in good stead. It brought the Moravians greater recognition and prestige in the eyes of European governments than mission societies could command. Moreover, in class-conscious Europe, the aristocratic leadership of the Unitas Fratrum, particularly in its early days, was an asset in dealing with officialdom.

But the most important contribution of the Moravians was their emphasis that every Christian is a missionary and should witness through his daily vocation. If the example of the Moravians had been studied more carefully by other Christians, it is possible that the businessman might have retained his honored place within the expanding Christian world mission beside the preacher, teacher, and physician.

The artisan was king in the eighteenth century, especially in overseas areas. Significant is the decision of a physician named Reynier in Pilgerhuth, Berbice, near Surinam, who decided in 1741 to shift to shoemaking since this brought in much more income.[10]

Missionary strategy was as decisive as economic considerations in choosing a vocation. The Brethren selected crafts rather than agriculture because these would give them greater mobility for the missions of the Lamb.[11] And the Moravians matched their artisan missionaries to appropriate fields. This was one reason for their overall success. Generally, the Brethren addressed themselves to primitive peoples. They came as simple artisans, working with and for the indigenous people, caring for both their physical and spiritual welfare. Usually, they left the advanced cultures to other missions.

The Industrial Revolution and its cheap, English factory goods[12] gradually undermined the Moravian dependence on the artisan missionary, who had often enjoyed a virtual monopoly in frontier settings. Abroad, the Industrial Revolution had the effect of making primitive areas the suppliers of cheap raw materials, and industry developed slowly there. At home, however, the Moravians kept pace with the Revolution. Building on the mercantile foundation of Abraham Dürninger, his successors developed impressive manufacturing enterprises in Herrnhut and Gnadenfrei, Silesia. But under the Communist regime of the German Democratic Republic, such enterprises have passed almost entirely out of Moravian control.

There has never been a lack of tension in the relation of mission and economic activities for the Moravians. Zinzendorf expressed his misgivings over one scheme after another.[13] Only three years before his death, he declared:

> We had thought that in the lands where the devil still lives the service of the Gospel could be combined with business. But now we have come to an entirely different conviction. And I hope that we will not think of it in this way any more.[14]

Does this mean that Zinzendorf was opposed in principle to missionaries' seeking an independent economic base? Hardly. Witness the abandon with which he sent out artisan missionaries.

But the Moravians did not limit themselves to Zinzendorf's inhibitions. In the very next year after Zinzendorf's criticism, Jonas Paul Weiss sent the Surinam mission a chest of striped linen for sale together with a strong plea to overcome false scruples and to begin supporting the mission by commerce.

By the late nineteenth century, a Moravian director of missions insisted that Moravian religious principles not only tolerate but *demand* the combination of commercial and missionary activities. He denounced any effort to regard certain activities as more Christian than others. The power of Christianity should fill all areas of life; they are not to be opposed to one another. The aim of Moravian missionaries is to lead the individual Christian to the sanctification of all areas of life. Therefore, they find nothing strange about being both missionaries and business people.[15]

The Moravians recognized, of course, that missions and economic activities each have their own inner dynamics and follow their own laws. But they did not take the easy way of resolving the tension by cutting off all connection between the two poles. Their Christian maturity revealed itself in their willingness to live with the tension. True, they occasionally learned through sad experience that it was damaging to both missions and economic activities, if these were mixed indiscriminately. But they had also learned that it could be equally bad for missions, if economic power was in unfriendly hands. They had learned that hostile plantation owners could keep them from evangelizing their slaves. Again, in Greenland the missionaries had suffered when the trading monopoly passed into the hands of Jacob Severin, a Jutland merchant, who had no heart for missions.[16]

Dedication to the Savior's cause helped them to distinguish missions from economics without separating them. Both were subordinated to the service of the Lamb. Fraternity in spirit united the Brethren in the discrete organizational entities of mission and business. Whatever their short-term objectives, the long-range goals were the same. The church organization of the Unitas Fratrum allowed the Moravians to succeed in keeping mission and economic activities distinct and yet united under the overall church order of the Unitas Fratrum. In spite of persisting tensions, the Unity of the Brethren hammered out a working unity of the spiritual and material aspects of the Christian world mission which has eluded most other missionary fellowships.

Part II

ECONOMIC ACTIVITIES
AND A MISSION SOCIETY:
THE BASEL MISSION TRADING COMPANY

XI

Beginnings of the Basel Mission Society

The year was 1815, a rather unlikely time for founding a missionary society. Napoleon had returned from exile, landing at Cannes on March 1. Terror gripped Europe, and three armies marched against the common foe. The decisive battle of Waterloo was fought on June 18, 1815, but the war went on. All summer the city of Basel heard the thunder of French cannon. And through the streets marched Russian armies made up of strange Mongol peoples whom the burghers of Basel hardly knew by name—Kalmuks, Bashkirs, Buriats—some partly Christianized, others frankly animistic pagans, and still others Moslems. It was these non-Christian peoples who became the saviors of Basel at the bombardment of nearby Hüningen. In a surge of gratitude toward God and their non-Christian deliverers, a group of Christian friends in Basel conceived the thought of demonstrating their thanks by showing these non-Christian people the gospel of eternal salvation. This first became concrete in the establishment of a small mission school.[1]

Though Basel is not a seaport, it had a long commercial tradition because of its strategic position for interior trade. To the farsighted-ness of Bishop Henry of Thun, the city owed the construction in 1225 of the first, and for centuries the only, firm bridge over the Rhine between the Bodensee and the sea. Both the Basel mercantile élan and the Basel pietist spirit helped to form the unique shape which the Basel mission enterprises took.[2]

Early in the eighteenth century, Basel had become an important center of pietistic influence. Moravians were in the picture; about 300 *Herrnhuter* were there by 1783. Already in 1780, under the influence of Johann August Urlsperger (1728-1806), pastor at Augsburg, a voluntary association had been formed at Basel which was first called the "German Christian Society" (*Deutsche Chris-tentumsgesellschaft*), but eventually came to be called the "German Society for the Promotion of Christian Truth and Piety."[3]

This was the launching pad for the Basel Mission Society,[4] which became a classic example of the mission-society approach as contrasted with the approach of the Moravians, who had shown the world a whole church body dedicated to missions.[5] Out of a number of mission societies which engaged in economic activities or formed sister organizations for that purpose, I have chosen Basel for typological reasons. No other mission society exhibits such an extensive and developed economic activity.[6]

Like the men of Herrnhut, the candidates were for the most part artisans.[7] Since the "Plan of the Mission Institute" approved by the committee on March 7, 1816, restricted enrollment to "pious men and youths who have reached their twentieth year," the students would normally be such as had mastered a trade.[8] The general theory was that every man of good character and sincere Christian purpose could be utilized somewhere, and it was the business of the Society to find out where. The first two groups trained in the new mission school at Basel comprised Wilhelm Dürr and Daniel Müller, stocking weavers of Fluntern, Peter Knecht, a factory worker from the Basel area, Bormeister, a glove maker of Kurland, Johann Ludwig Irion of Alpirsbach, shoemaker, Dreher, rope maker, and Winkler of Württemberg, a scrivener, the only white collar worker in the lot.[9]

The Basel Mission effort did not originally intend to send out missionaries on its own. Its purpose was to establish a training school for missionaries similar to the one carried on by Johannes Jänicke (1748-1827) in Berlin. Some of his graduates entered the service of the London Missionary Society and the Church Missionary Society. Jänicke himself had been appointed by the London Missionary Society to head its activities in Germany. However, Jänicke's school in Berlin had been hindered in its work by the Napoleonic Wars. The more neutral situation in Switzerland was regarded as preferable. This proved to be a farsighted decision. Even so, the Basel Mission

Society's strong German ties were to have fateful consequences in the twentieth century.

The man finally chosen to head the new mission institute at Basel was Christian Gottlieb Blumhardt (1779-1838), son of a shoemaker, theologically trained and then pastor at Bürg in Württemberg. He was no stranger to Basel, having served there from 1803 to 1807 as secretary of the *Christentumsgesellschaft.*

In Blumhardt's call, it was significantly stated that the graduates were to "spread a beneficent civilization" and "proclaim the Gospel of peace." This very aptly describes the unique combination of spiritual and economic activities carried on by later graduates of the mission institute in Basel. Though the Society depended over-whelmingly on the freewill offerings of pietist friends for support, it is interesting in view of later commercial enterprises to note that from the beginning the "Plan of the Mission Institute" expressed the hope that additional help might come from "the profits from mission publications."[10]

Blumhardt showed at once that he was a man worth the salary he had held out for.[11] By July 1816, only three months after moving to Basel, he was on the market with the first issue of *Magazin für die neueste Geschichte der protestantischen Missions- und Bibel-gesellschaften: Eine Zeitschrift für Freunde des Christentums und der Menschheit.* Its impressive scope of 152 pages gave the editor elbow room to be both learned and popular.[12] He also made money. From 1823 to 1839, the total profit was 37,088 francs.[13] At his death, this magazine and the later *Heidenbote* supported the mission school completely.[14]

In its subtitle the new *Magazin* was making its appeal not only to Christians but also to humanitarians. This fact, among others, indicates that right from the beginning the men of Basel were concerned about this world as well as the next. Most important, perhaps, was the traditional makeup of its missionary force, most of them men who had worked with their hands and had mastered a trade.

Already by 1821 the Basel Society had moved beyond the mere training of missionaries for other groups and actually sent some of them out under its own auspices, in the first instance beyond the Caucasus in southern Russia. Here in a number of mission colonies, whose life involved them in social as well as religious concerns, fourteen Basel trainees were serving.[15] The Basel men ministered

especially to 500 German families in new colonies in the Tiflis area.
Beyond this, a special mission colony was founded in the Karabagh
area at Schusha among Armenian Christians. The purpose was to
reach Muslims by revitalizing the Christians of the ancient Oriental
church. Schools, teacher training, conferences with younger Armenian clergy, and literature produced by their own print shop were the
means employed. When a Scottish mission gave up its Russian work,
their mission colony fell to the Basel men, but this involved the
missionaries in a great many problems that did not advance their
religious work. Many Tartar converts were interested in joining the
colony but were repelled by problems inherited from the Scots.
In 1835 a ukase from St. Petersburg put an abrupt end to the Basel
Mission in Russia. But already this first abortive effort in Russia had
shown that the men of Basel were not ready to confine themselves
to so-called "spiritual" affairs in mission work.

XII

Economic Activities in India

When the practical artisans of Basel, now ordained, began their work in India in 1834, it was to be expected that they would continue to be practical also in their approach to mission problems.

In the Tamil country each caste lived in a separate community, and the people were often converted by whole villages. In such circumstances the whole social and economic structure remained intact, and the missionary had no need to provide the converts with new homes and trades.

But the people of the Malabar coast are to the present day more individualistic. Each family had its own house and compound. Villages with rows of houses were scarce. The Basel Mission community there was formed by individuals and small families coming out and seeking shelter under the missionary's protection. Hence the problems were 1) to find a dwelling; 2) to find work to meet their daily needs; and 3) to teach the converts to start a new way of life.

When the Basel missionaries succeeded at last in winning some converts in India, many of these were ostracized from their caste and cut off from family, friends, employers, property, and livelihood. On the one hand, this resulted in a unique casteless community forming around the gospel, for numerous castes were represented in the Basel Mission, a factor which set it apart from other Christian missions. On the other hand, it confronted the Basel missionaries with the urgent economic needs of these fellow Christians who had paid such a high

84   PROFIT FOR THE LORD

price for their new-found faith. One could not simply let them starve, and to put them forever on a missionary dole would not be good for their sense of human dignity and freedom.

The Christian church historically has felt most at home with agricultural answers to economic problems. This also shaped the first attempt by the Basel missionaries. Baptized Christians and catechumens were formed into Christian villages farming mission lands. Some lands were given by the government outright or in perpetual lease; some were the gifts of English benefactors. Others were purchased at a small price by the mission. But these farm lands were a source of endless irritation, frustration, and trouble for the mission. Very little was accomplished. The majority of the people were totally unaccustomed to regular work, even to farm work, and the ordained missionaries often lacked the time and the interest to supervise the farms. There was some improvement after 1859 when special business managers were assigned to each district who also became responsible for the farms. General agent Gottlob Pfleiderer could report to the general conference in 1861, "It is a great blessing that the missionaries no longer have to fight with the people all week and then preach to them of love on Sunday."[1]

At the local level the ordained missionary was still in the picture. And this led to constant problems. The effort to develop a self-respecting peasant class failed. No matter how low the land rent was placed, in many cases the Indian Christian peasant did not even intend to pay it. For he knew perfectly well that the land was mission property, and that the church would never be so demanding as an ordinary Indian landlord. The missionaries were forced to drive out lazy Christians and put heathen tenants in their place in order to prevent further losses. Frequently, catechumens were brought into this agricultural project, money was loaned to them, and when they could not pay, they were foreclosed. The mission must have seemed to many of them like a moneylender who advances funds in order to ruin his debtors and take their property. It seemed to follow the general Indian viewpoint which regards the capital as a total loss from the beginning and therefore demands very high interest. Where the lands were the property of the local congregations, as in Mangalore, the Christians took a dim view of further conversions, because each household's share of the acreage would be reduced thereby. Entirely aside from the fluctuations in the profit factor in the plantations, the mission was embarrassed to find itself regarded by the people as a financial institution and a business enterprise. Many of the people despised the mission because the missionary was a planter and, on top of that, one to whom they were indebted.[2]

Although the agricultural effort undoubtedly brought blessings to some Christians, it is understandable that Otto Schott, who as Basel mission inspector visited India in 1880 and 1881, should render this verdict on the 2,620 acres in south Mahratta: "Our colossal property in India is a lead weight, which paralyzes mission work, a mildew on the proclamation of the Gospel, and the incubus which holds down the spiritual life of our congregations."[3] Of course, Schott was opposed to every kind of close connection between missions and economic activities; eventually he resigned his post as inspector over the issue, as we shall see.

Since Basel had spoken, the case was finished. Most of the mission lands in India were sold or returned to the government. But significantly, the Indian Christians, whose opinion no one had apparently asked, deplored the sale of the mission plantations which they considered "the glory of the mission."[4]

There were apparently no attempts to set up Christian peasants as owners rather than tenants of farm land. This is in marked contrast to the path taken in agricultural missions by the Basel missionaries in Africa. There, as we shall see, the newly introduced cocoa bean was placed in the hands of small, independent African farmers. Such an approach greatly strengthened the development of this entire sector of society. However, what was possible in the rather primitive culture of Africa with cocoa may not have been possible in India with the cultivation of rice and other grains, which require a much more sophisticated treatment. The cultivation of cereals has to be done on a large scale to be profitable and therefore requires large capital support. Even today, land redistribution has not everywhere proved successful (Japan is a notable exception), and may not be the universal answer.

But already long before Otto Schott became disenchanted with mission plantations in India, other missionaries had begun to suspect that agriculture did not hold all the answers to the economic needs of the Indian people. One missionary wrote to Inspector Hoffmann already in 1842: "The more our work expands, the more urgent becomes the question whether our congregations will not become a great weight for the mission unless they learn trades."[5]

The mission school at Mangalore devoted afternoons to hand-craft, including weaving. There was also an industrial school, for

which teacher J. F. Metz had a big carpet loom made because carpets
enjoyed a ready sale to the British in India. The children worked in
the afternoon. He hoped to pay for all the looms in two years by the
sale of the products. Already he was weaving enough cloth for all the
boys in the school. Bookbinding was also done. But he was having
trouble with the native smith and hoped for an artisan from Basel.[6]

The result was that the mission board in 1846 sent two clock-
makers, Rösinger and Müller, to Mangalore to introduce the
manufacture of Black Forest cuckoo clocks and to train boys of the
congregation as apprentices. But American competition in large
clocks was too stiff;[7] watchmaking, too, proved unsuccessful. In the
land of timelessness there was no great demand for timepieces.[8]

The mission board was learning a lesson in cultural differences,
and ventured:

> a converted Hindu is far from being a European . . . and the
> civilization that has been handed down to us through a
> millennium and a half is a product of the Gospel and a gift of
> special divine grace, which gives us also in industrial capabili-
> ties a seldom measured headstart.[9]

There was a whole series of failures: silk culture, arrowroot,
cocoanut oil. Nothing seemed to get anywhere.

The first success was an enterprise indispensable to many an
overseas mission—a print shop and bindery. Beginning with a small
hand press in 1841, the Basel Mission Press by the decade of
1864-1873 was producing 322 books and pamphlets in almost a
million copies. The *Madras Mail* in 1873 said that the Basel Mission
Press did the best work in the entire Madras Presidency. For years
the government examinations were entrusted to it, and not once was
there any indiscretion, in a land where even government school
inspectors are often bribed to reveal copies ahead of time. The press
employed forty to fifty workers. A printer from Württemberg,
Georg Plebst, had taken over the enterprise in 1851. And from then
on the print shop had been under professional supervision. It was an
international effort. A Chinese named Tommy Luklin was trained by
Plebst to fashion typefaces. (Kanarese requires 240 characters.) The
press made its Christian witness not only through first-class work
and through honesty, but also through the type of non-Christian
literature which it produced. Expurgated Indian historical publications were published. And the Basel Mission Press succeeded in

holding down somewhat the rise of presses producing obscene literature.[10] Regularly, a dozen apprentices were in training. They were housed in a dormitory and received Christian training.[11]

A bindery soon employed thirty workers. In the course of time this could be given over to an Indian.[12] This man's story shows dramatically how the Basel Mission brought a new life in many dimensions to some of the people of India. His name was Luke Joshua, a "mentally and physically very competent" employee of Plebst. He paid off the bindery machines in two years and then erected new buildings to house the enterprise, employing nearly thirty people.[13] At first people were jealous of him and refused to give him their sons as apprentices. He gladly took widows and very poor boys, even boys in poor health assigned him by the presbytery. Later the members of the congregation repented of their pride, and many young men learned book binding from him. Luke Joshua tried to serve other church members through his business.

Woodworking and carpentry was another branch of Basel industry. Again in 1856 Basel sent out a trained, experienced man, who was both cabinet maker and carpenter. Three years later he already kept thirty workers and apprentices busy. At times the number went to ninety, when there were churches to build for the mission or other structures for cash customers.

But there were problems. The inner drive of the business and the objectives of the mission resulted in a conflict of interests. The missionary imperative demanded training as many apprentices as possible and making them independent artisans. Business interests would have required limiting the number sharply and choosing workers on the basis of their ability without considering the needs of the Christian congregations. Besides, as more apprentices were trained, native competition became more severe. In addition, other Europeans entered the field. However, the missionary purpose was gratifyingly fulfilled in that numerous young people had become independent artisans and now could earn their own bread.[14]

But it was in weaving and tile-making that the Basel industries gradually got beyond the small shop approach in India. Already in 1846 a missionary at Mangalore, the oldest Basel station, had imported a European loom. This, however, was different from trying to make German cuckoo clocks in India. For there was an indigenous, though primitive weaving industry on which the missionaries could build. In 1851 a master weaver, John Haller, was sent out to exploit the opportunities that beckoned. After nineteen months he already had more than twenty looms at which twenty-seven workers, including six apprentices, were employed. By 1856 their skill had progressed so far that the Basel looms won second prize at an industrial fair at Madras.[15]

John Haller may have left his mark on world history when he sought a dye for his cloth that would withstand the burning Indian sun and the torture test of the Indian *dhobi,* or launderer. He experimented with the sap of the bark of the semecarpus tree, and here found the color that came to clothe the marching men of many nations. He gave his new color the Kanarese name "khaki," which means "dusty," because it looks like the ubiquitous brownish yellow dust of the Indian road.[16] It was an instantaneous success. The police chief of Mangalore was so enthusiastic that he clothed his entire police force in this color. And on a visit to the Basel Mission weaving establishment at Balmatha, Lord Roberts of Kandahar, then Commander-in-Chief of Her Majesty's forces, was so impressed with the practicality of this cloth that, it is said, he emphatically recommended its introduction into the British Army, which followed. And so it may be that from this humble mission beginning, khaki began its march around the world.[17]

The Basel looms had other, more local, successes. An indestructible cloth, originally made for hunting, came to be called "Webster's Shikaree," after the Englishman who had first ordered it. So close-woven that it could keep out the sharp tips of grass and the omnipresent dust of the Indian terrain, this cloth became immensely popular.[18]

By 1880 there were one hundred workers. Of these about half were widows and other women who had to support themselves. Without the looms they would have become a burden on the mission. The social circumstances of many workers had so improved that many of them who had once lived in miserable huts now had healthful, cheerful cottages of their own with a small garden. The consciousness that they had some modest property of their own did much to make their life more worth living. This is something the tenants on the Basel plantations had never attained, and perhaps there is a lesson to be drawn from this comparison.[19] There was a credit union and a health insurance plan into which employees were required to deposit up to 6 per cent of their wages.[20] Contrary to the opinion of most dyed-in-the-wool missionaries, mission boards

are not always wrong. It was the industrial commission of the board
in Basel that in 1867 insisted on the credit unions—something
unheard of in India. The missionaries themselves regarded these
credit unions as utterly unfeasible in improvident, debt-ridden India.
But Basel gave the orders, and to the amazement of the missionaries,
the credit unions succeeded.[21]

As time went on, branches of the weaving industry were started
in many other places. Daily devotions were held in each of these
establishments by the European superintendent. Experience showed
that this agreed very well with the strict working standards on which
he insisted; both together had an educational influence on the
people.[22] The workers were mostly Christians, but non-Christians
were also employed if they did not actively oppose the Christian
spirit and intention of those establishments.

But if the Christians of the Basel Mission were not to become just
another weaver caste, they would have to diversify their employment. Tile manufacture proved to be the solution. It was the
successful printer Georg Plebst who moved out beyond his own
trade and took the initiative. On a furlough in Switzerland, Plebst
suggested pottery and tile-making to the industrial commission and
offered to use his furlough to study pottery and glazing in Germany.
The commission advanced modest capital. The clay in the Mangalore
area proved very suitable. But there were serious disappointments.
Finally, with English money Plebst made one last attempt. And this
time, in late 1865, he succeeded. His kiln and his products soon
excelled all others in the land.[23] The plenipotentiary of the British
government was so impressed with the quality of Plebst's roof tile
that he ordered the entire next year's production in advance and
commanded its use on all new government buildings as far as it
would reach. Now expansion capital was needed badly. Happily,
right at this time the Balmatha weaving establishments were paying
back their loans and the money could be reinvested in the tile works.
New and improved production facilities brought a medal of honor
from the British government for Basel Mission tiles. They were less
porous than native tiles, an important factor in the monsoon season;
and they weighed less, which made construction substantially
cheaper. By 1873 the tile works had repaid all the capital that had
been advanced.

In 1876 Plebst, who had become an invalid, was replaced by
Jacob Baumann, a Swiss tiler with a superb technical background.

The opening of the "Arakullu Tiling Establishment," a branch at Calicut (now Khoznikode), on the Malabar coast, falls into this era. In Mangalore the profitable business brought competition, with Englishmen and Catholics entering the field. But the men of Basel met the challenge by increasing their production. And then native princes began to order Christian tiles. Even the old Zamorin, the native prince of Calicut, ordered a large quantity of tiles after he had persuaded himself there was no magical danger in the firm's stamp, "Basel Mission Tile Works."[24]

The various industries required the presence of a European mechanic. Karl Hüttinger was sent out in 1871. He not only kept the looms and the tile works going, but he trained apprentices as well. And while he also accepted outside contracts for the building of pumps, houses, and bridges, his chief service remained achieving the original purpose of the mission workshops—training independent artisans who could earn their own livelihood.[25]

In 1853 Gottlob Pfleiderer was sent out as missionary merchant. How happy the missionaries were to find needed supplies for house and school in his store. For the industrial enterprise, which had production technicians but lacked commercial know-how, Pfleiderer became both purchasing agent and sales manager. Pfleiderer failed, however, in his attempts to train apprentices in his stores. The temptation to pilfer articles from the shelves proved too strong for people who had been accustomed for ages to different ethical standards.[26]

Pfleiderer's shops were a successful demonstration of Christian honesty in other respects, however. The non-Christian Indians marvelled to see that he sold his goods at firm prices. He had only "one word." A child could buy goods for exactly the same price as a grown man![27]

To this day corruption is a way of life in much of Asia, just as it is in the so-called Christian West whenever living Christian faith disappears. The Basel Mission industries showed that there is a better way. For example, in 1869 the collector for Mangalore discovered that the official revenue stamps had been altered and that for years a conspiracy of higher Indian officials and wealthier citizens had swindled the government out of large sums. Now the collector wanted to transfer the entire sale of revenue stamps to the Basel Mission trading department—and it accepted a large proportion of it.

This incident became a testimonial to the ethical concerns of Christianity.[28]

By 1894 the industrial establishments of the Basel Mission in India brought in a profit of over 4,640 francs, although this was never their chief object.[29] Or, to give the big picture, while expenditures for India remained stable at a little less than 350,000 francs for each of three decades ending 1874, 1884, and 1894, income on the mission field, nearly all of it from the industries and trade, stood at 74,000, 64,000 and 93,000 francs, respectively.[30] On the eve of World War I, in 1913, the Basel industrial enterprises in India had become a big business complex, employing 3,636 persons.[31]

But not everyone was in agreement with this adoption of factory methods and mass production. Tile manufacture had gotten off to such a fast start that there had never been much opportunity to debate the issue. Customers had been overjoyed to find a product superior to the heavy, inefficient indigenous Indian tile.[32] Both the demand for Basel Mission tile and the quick rise of competitors required the Basel missionary tilemakers to join the Industrial Revolution by installing steam power and mass production facilities. It is significant that they kept pace. The era of the artisan missionary was at an end.[33]

But in textile weaving, the conversion to factory methods was slower. All concerned were reluctant to turn from the hand loom to the factory system, for they feared the adverse impact that mass production could have on working conditions and congregational life. However, competition forced their hand.

In 1914 a significant debate on factory methods versus hand weaving took place when the board set up its budget for the year. Certain village hand weaving establishments were to be closed in favor of a centrally located factory at Quilandy near Calicut. But various voices warned against the concentration and proletarianizing of the Christian hand weavers in the industrial city.[34]

The main points of that debate are instructive. Inspector Theodore Oehler, who served from 1884 to 1915, advanced a most unrealistic proposal: "Could one not subsidize the hand weavers, who are now working at a loss, from the profits of the textile factory?" But the merchants on the board pointed out that factory products cost only half as much as the textiles woven on small hand and house looms. The latter had no future. Only factory production held out any hope to the Indian for earning his livelihood. Moreover, the Basel merchants argued, work which continues to be unprofitable has no ethical value. They conceded that in the eyes of some Christians it is more pious to close with a loss, but contended that the Christian businessman could not allow himself the luxury of such thoughts.[35]

One spokesman was moved by this instructive dialogue between theologians and merchants to regard the entire India mission as an artificial plant in so far as it depended on mission industries. He urged helping the Indian Christians to become independent artisans or helping them earn their bread in some other independent fashion.

Mission leaders were not alone in raising the nostalgic hope of a return to the day of the independent artisan. A little later Gandhi would raise the same ideal of cottage industry in India. But while this might give very limited help to the village peasant in the off-season, it would not solve the problem of earning an adequate living in an industralized age. His handcraft would have increasing difficulty competing with cheap factory goods. Many of Gandhi's co-workers and successors would regard his ideals of cottage industry as a burden in their endeavors to industralize and thereby meet the challenge of famine and the population explosion.

Meanwhile, centralized industries in the Basel Mission also made possible the formation of numerically strong congregations. Already by 1909 Mangalore had a congregation of 3,000 souls, unusual in non-Christian India with its many small and weak village churches.

XIII

Economic Activities in Africa

The Basel enterprises in Africa were even larger and certainly more profitable than those in India. The first four Basel missionaries arrived on the Gold Coast in December 1828, when the Danes held the fort of Christiansborg. But they soon learned why this coast was called "the white man's grave." Within the single month of August 1829, three out of the four young missionaries died. And by the end of 1831, the fourth was dead too. (Earlier, the Gold Coast had defeated even the indomitable Moravians, who after three attempts in the eighteenth century had nothing to show but the graves of their missionaries.)

Words fail one to describe the Christian heroism with which three Basel volunteers at once came forward to take the place of those who had fallen. Few battlefields of history have exhibited a greater willingness to die than that demonstrated by Christian missionaries in many parts of Africa. These were the dying words of someone on another field: "Don't give up Africa! Let a thousand more missionaries die, but don't stop sending." After Adlai Stevenson visited Africa and saw numerous missionary headstones he exclaimed, "My God, the graves! The graves all over Africa!"

The second Basel group of three included a medical doctor; but he was the first to die—within forty-four days of landing in Christiansborg on March 13, 1832. By July 18 the second had followed. The third lay at death's door in September with yellow jaundice—but he was pulled through by a native African "doctor" who treated him with cold baths. A European merchant named Lutterodt proved his sincere friendship for the missionaries by inviting him to his country home for rest and rehabilitation. In 1840, after twelve years, this missionary, Andreas Riis, was still the sole survivor of nine Basel volunteers. One is speechless at the quiet heroism of a Moravian bride who came to join Riis in 1837—and lived only to 1845.

The story of the Basel Mission in Africa almost throughout the nineteenth century can be told, then, in death notices. Yet in 1850, when many were wondering whether Africa should be given up, whether the Basel Mission school trainees would still have the courage to go to Africa and to almost certain death, the whole graduating class volunteered! The inspector told the general conference on July 4, 1850: "Our Lord did not redeem the world without dying, and the mission cannot be carried on unless those who dedicate themselves to it are ready to die."

Many of the Basel trainees who went out to die on the Gold Coast were not ordained. They manned the mission's trading posts. But by their heroic faith and sacrificial death they earned the same respect that Christians show the ordained missionaries who are buried beside them. The Basel Trading Company, as it is known today, lost fifty-eight men overseas between 1862 and 1956, almost all in Africa, and thirty-seven before the turn of the century. Most died within a few years of arrival on the Gold Coast.[1]

Of course, the number of preaching missionaries who gave their lives must have been far greater than the number of missionary merchants and other employees of the Trading Company. There are many missionary graves in the cemetery at Christiansborg, Accra. Reliable overall figures show that by 1919 no fewer than 145 people out of the 569 sent to the Gold Coast by the Basel Mission had died because of the climate.[2]

The mortality rate among Basel missionaries led to an attempt to draw in missionaries of other races and places who would not be quite so vulnerable to the deadly Gold Coast climate. This may be of interest in an age when mission leaders speak more and more of a mission based on six continents and aimed at six continents, while non-Western churches are sending out hundreds of their own missionaries, proving that a white skin is not a prerequisite for missionary service. Inspector Wilhelm Hoffmann advanced the unique plan of sending a small colony of West Indian Negro

Christians to the Gold Coast. They were recruited among the Moravian Christians, with whom the men of Basel felt a close spiritual bond. After overcoming countless difficulties and endless red tape, missionaries brought six families and two youths from Jamaica and another from Antigua, twenty-four people in all, to the Gold Coast on Easter Sunday, 1843. However, it was in general a disappointing experience from the evangelistic standpoint. The "immigrants" were often arrogant and lazy, and did not provide an attractive picture of Christianity. Some of their descendants, however, served the church well.[3]

The cultural contributions of the West Indian Moravians were, perhaps, of greater value. They brought along many useful plants. Coffee and tobacco plantations resulted; arrowroot and all kinds of tropical fruits, such as oranges and mangos, were planted. Coffee plantations and mango trees spread through the whole region.[4]

Like the self-supporting Moravian artisans, some of the artisan missionaries of Basel went out with the firm intention to provide for their own livelihood.[5] Industry never attained the scope in Africa that it achieved in India. In the Asian country it was a case of having to rescue people economically who had, as it were, lost their membership in the human race by being expelled from their caste. But in Africa the task was to work for the moral, religious, and cultural development of a nonindustrial people and to bridge the wide cultural gap between Europeans and Africans. After sacrificial efforts with shoemaking, pottery, straw plaiting, and cattle raising, the only lasting results were achieved with a combined wood-working and metal-working shop in Christiansborg. It never became a large-scale enterprise, but it solved a number of difficult problems. It assisted the mission in its many operations, lifted the housing standards for the Africans, and accustomed many of them to regular work. It created a class of respected artisans. Everywhere on the west coast, the former apprentices of the mission shops were in demand. Africans came to appreciate the importance of solid preparation for a craft. And it was to be had virtually nowhere but in the mission shops, where everything from light hand wagons to iron bridges was built. But the training of apprentices was the chief dividend.[6]

But unlike in India, trade became the chief activity of the commercial missionaries from Basel. It all started with the desire to provide necessary supplies to the missionaries at stations in the hinterland. There were no postal or railroad services until the beginning of the twentieth century, and everything had to be transported by carriers. This was a kind of diaconate to spare the ordained missionary's time and strength for the ministry of Word and Sacrament in church and school. In time, the *Speditionsbruder* in Christiansborg would have to prepare from 200 to 300 headloads per month, each weighing sixty pounds: provisions, house furnishings and kitchen equipment, cloth, needles and thread, tools, and building materials such as lime, cement, and tar.[7] Eventually the practice arose of back-loading indigenous products such as palm nuts and palm oil in order to help pay the high costs of such human transport. This led inevitably to trading posts in a far-flung network through present-day Ghana and Cameroun.[8]

The man who laid the foundations for what became an empire of missionary commerce was Hermann Rottmann of Altona, first sent out in late 1854 as the forwarding agent in Christiansborg. Soon he became the general treasurer of the Basel Mission. Rottmann clearly looked upon himself not just as a merchant but as a missionary. His father writes that he went to Africa because "he could no longer resist proclaiming the Gospel of our Lord Jesus Christ to the heathen sunken in spiritual and physical misery." This rugged, twenty-two-year-old missionary merchant, who worked for forty-three amazing years in the land of death, soon saw other possibilities for employing his merchandising experience. He wrote a letter to the mission board at Basel asking for permission to open a shop in Christiansborg, because he saw the chance to make a "good profit" for the mission society. The idea from Africa found the groundwork already laid in Basel. Already two years earlier, the silk-ribbon manufacturer Daniel Burckhardt-Forcart (1805-1879) had offered the new industrial commission of the board a loan of 5000 francs for just such a purpose. He provided the financial nest egg that hatched a great enterprise.[9]

However, the mission board admonished Rottmann not to be just another trader. His little shop should be "an oasis in the immense desert of heathenism," and support and strengthen the growing Christian congregation. Significantly, he was to train helpers in the business, even if that took time. Inspector Josenhans and the merchant Sarasin, who at the time were responsible for this new department of mission activities, reminded Rottmann that he was not carrying on a fly-by-night business, but establishing a permanent enterprise. They expressed the hope that this commercial activity serving the mission would forever be united with the latter.[10]

By 1912 the Gold Coast trade employed 634 Europeans and 566 Africans. For a time the Basel Mission Trading Company had its own river steamer in Africa, and between 1866 and 1885 had, like the Moravians in the Labrador trade, five vessels of its own sailing between Christiansborg and Bremerhaven, bringing to Africa missionary supplies and trade goods and returning to Europe with palm products, cotton, rubber, coffee from mission plantations, and other indigenous produce. But when regular steamship service came into being, the Trading Company sold the last of its sailing ships. For all its sacred objectives, the Trading Company was not spared any of the hazards that beset commercial enterprises, including storms, shipwrecks, native rebellions, war, financial crises, unworthy employees, and even disappointing European agents who had to be dismissed. But it weathered them all, and through the years made invaluable contributions to the entire area in which it operated.

The Company played an important role in the introduction of cocoa into Ghana. Cocoa was indigenous not to Africa, but to South America. Three Swiss farmers, members of the Basel Mission, were the first to plant cocoa in what is now Ghana.[11] And in 1879, Tetteh Quarshie, an African slave whose freedom Basel missionaries had purchased from a Fante man, brought cocoa beans from Fernando Po and San Thome, islands in the Bay of Biafra, where Spanish planters grew it on large plantations with contract laborers. Another missionary, Arnold Mohr, imported cocoa pods from the Camerouns in 1889. The British government, which followed the Danes in control of the Gold Coast, also promoted cocoa planting in cooperation with Basel missionaries. The Trading Company shipped its first consignment of cocoa to Europe in 1891.[12] By 1911 the total production in Ghana reached 40 million kilograms, and cocoa had become, for good and for ill, the economic monoculture of Ghana. In fact, within two decades Ghana had become the leading cocoa producing country in all the world. For many years, half the world's cocoa crop was grown there. As the mission workshops had helped create an independent class of artisans, so the mission trading company and its agricultural efforts helped to create and strengthen an independent class of African farmers.

Already in 1902 it was clear that the Trading Company saw in cocoa not primarily a means of making money but a means of helping people realize themselves as free and independent children of God. The men of Basel paid tribute to the British government for its wise policy of encouraging the small independent cocoa farmer rather than the plantation system, which they saw as only one level above slavery. As independent cocoa farmers, the Africans proved the contention of the Basel missionaries that Africans were not naturally lazy but would work on their own without outside pressure—so long as they received the full fruit of their labors.[13] It was additional evidence that the productive gifts and capacities of the people of Asia and Africa would not be released in full measure unless these people could be masters in their own commercial enterprises and profit fully from them. The incursion of European culture awakened in the African a whole series of new wants, and he worked hard to satisfy them. Industrious German and Swiss missionary businessmen conceded that Africans at times not only equalled but exceeded their own performances.[14] However, though cocoa culture has given Ghana the highest per capita income of any nation in Africa, except South Africa, material wealth in any society is never an unmixed blessing.[15] But the new flow of cocoa money enabled Christians of the Basel Mission Society to contribute the handsome total of $26,000 to the church as early as 1910.[16]

Hermann L. Rottmann is credited with bringing the Gold Coast another source of income. Until his time palm nuts were thrown away as worthless or used as fuel. But by the first decade of the twentieth century, dozens of steamers were filling their holds with them, annually bringing large sums of money into the country, and benefitting the women and children especially, since they handled the preparation and transport of these nuts.[17]

The Trading Company also improved communications. It built roads into the interior and was the first to bring a truck to Ghana, already in 1908. Today this has grown into a large motor agency.

During the nineteenth century, the gin, schnapps, and gunpowder trade flourished on the west coast of Africa with all its evil influence on tribal wars and the slave trade, which was at first open, later clandestine. The gunpowder trade was chiefly in British hands. The gin and schnapps were chiefly of Dutch and German origin. German sources claim that in 1884 spirits composed 66 per cent of all the exports from Hamburg to West Africa.[18] In Ghana the Trading Company could offer formidable resistance to this trade. In fact, it could rightfully claim that by virtue of its unquestioned supremacy it could set the tone for the area, lending moral support to other German traders who were refusing to import spirits. By combining with these honorable German firms, the Basel Mission Trading Company succeeded in driving the liquor trade out of the area.[19]

Nonetheless, the company became more and more exposed to such severe competition by the firms indulging in the liquor trade, that its very existence was eventually threatened. Had the company, under this pressure, ceased to operate, its business would inevitably have fallen into the hands of these competitors. This danger stimulated the company to struggle on in spite of serious financial crises.[20]

Employment in the Trading Company sometimes gave dismissed seminarians, catechists, and other church workers who had proved unworthy a fresh start at a very critical point in their lives. Here they found moral influence and stability such as was not available elsewhere on the entire coast. Two of Africa's ablest pastors came from this group.[21] And throughout, the company continued to serve as the quartermaster corps giving logistic support to the evangelistic penetration of the hinterland by the missionaries. It provided all missionary supplies on the Gold Coast at cost plus a 5 per cent handling charge. This saved the mission about 10,000 francs a year, to say nothing of the time and frustration they were spared by the company's prompt and convenient service. The company took care of currency exchange, forwarded mail, and made itself responsible for the endless details connected with the arrival and departure of missionaries.

The commercial efforts were, however, part and parcel of the real mission work, not merely an appendage to it. They provided a graphic illustration in daily affairs of the power of the gospel at work in the hearts of Europeans and Africans who were concerned about demonstrating "faith active in love" not only in church services but also, where it may matter even more, in the market place and on the plantation. The lay missionaries built a solid reputation for dependable Christian character, becoming a model for many Africans.

The British government, predominant on the Gold Coast, bought Christiansborg from the Danes in 1850. But London had so little interest in the region at that time that the government was on the point of giving it up. At this moment of crisis, Elias Schrenk, first sent out as general treasurer of the Basel Mission, used his furlough in 1865 at the request of the mission administration to plead for the Gold Coast. The memorandum which he submitted to the Parliamentary Commission investigating the governmental system of the Gold Coast helped significantly, to the end that England, at the decisive moment, did not give up the Gold Coast. While he was at it, Schrenk lectured and gathered funds throughout England for the extension of the roads which the Basel Mission was building in order to develop the human and natural resources of the land he loved. Above all, he appealed to Britain to establish peace between the warring tribes. The Gold Coast stayed British, and though the government did little enough, it did give the missions—not only Basel but the Methodists—elbow room for their invaluable service to the people.[22]

Significantly, neither the Germans nor, of course, the Swiss exercised political control over the two areas where the Basel Mission commerce was centered. And when Elias Schrenk entered into political matters, he did not seek the colonial control of the Gold Coast for his own country. He sought to keep an indifferent and disinterested England on the job. Stephen Neill discusses Schrenk's work in his recent survey, *Colonialism and Christian Missions.*[23] Though he terms it "one of the clearest examples, in the whole of history, of cooperation between missionaries and a colonial government," he concludes, "It would be hard, on the basis of Schrenk's memorandum, to make out a case for the view that the missionaries were imperialistic in any ordinary sense of that term."

XIV

Organization and Contributions
of the Basel Enterprises

The Basel industries could never have attained their large scope if they had not been centrally organized and directed. Historians generally give 1852 as the year in which a separate industrial commission answerable to the mission board was organized. However, the beginnings actually go back to 1846, when the two clock-makers, Müller and Rösinger, were sent out. The mission board immediately set about creating a special commission to supervise this new work. All the historians, Eppler, Schlatter and Wanner, have overlooked this early beginning because they followed the later printed Reports instead of the earlier hand-written minutes of the Industrial Commission.[1]

On his trip to India in 1851-1852, Inspector Joseph Josenhans was strengthened in his conclusion that industrial enterprise had to be part of mission for Basel. And upon his return, he placed vigorous emphasis on this work. As a result, the Commission took a new lease on life in 1852. It now was only half as large but twice as effective, and included the mission director, Inspector Josenhans himself,[2] Karl Sarasin, a ribbon manufacturer who was a new board member, and the office manager. The Commission soon took an important step in 1853 by sending out to India someone who knew his business, the merchant Gottlob Pfleiderer.

The personal backing of Josenhans meant much for progress.

Josenhans and Sarasin were no mere activists. They had carefully thought out the reasons for their activity, and told the early industrial and commercial missionaries that their assignment included everything that could be done through industrial and commercial means for the welfare of the mission and the furtherance of the Kingdom of God. They were not only to provide a means of livelihood to the occasional needy Indian convert who had given up his caste and with it his means of subsistence, but they were to offer an example of Christian diligence, honesty, and reliability. Not only the church members at Mangalore but eventually those at all stations should be helped in this way. The hope was also expressed that a profit might result for the mission treasury.[3]

In a letter sent out to all the India mission stations on 1 February 1854 to explain the work of the Industrial Commission, Josenhans and Sarasin further refined the objectives. By this time they interpreted the Commission no longer merely as an aid to missions, but as a mission itself, "a mission not through preaching" but "through the power of example, through a model of Christianity revealing itself in practical life situations; . . . a mission doing everything possible to make it visible that godliness is profitable to all things, having promise not only for the life to come, but already for this present one."[4] With rare humility they recognized how difficult was the task they had set themselves, how hard it would be for them to get rid of attitudes shaped by their European culture and place themselves into the situation, the capabilities, and views of "a people upon whom the word of the Savior shines for the first time."[5]

The wistful hopes which Josenhans and Sarasin occasionally expressed for a possible income for the mission treasury were by no means their chief objective in industrial and commercial work. However, those hopes are understandable in view of the chronic fiscal deficits which dogged the Basel Mission Society during the middle of the nineteenth century. The crisis reached an acute climax in 1852, the year in which Josenhans himself took a hand in the *Industrie-Commission*. The mission board had to mortgage the *Missionshaus* itself as security for a loan of 55,000 French francs.[6] In spite of the financial crisis, 12,000 gulden of borrowed money were entrusted to the *Industrie-Commission* to give new Christians in India a chance to learn trades. This sum, it was recognized, would return only slowly, if ever. However, it was bread cast upon the waters, and it would return a hundredfold after many days.[7]

The arrival of an able and experienced businessman in India in the person of Gottlob Pfleiderer made a noticeable difference at once. Under his experienced guidance both trade and industry prospered. This led in 1859 to the founding of a separate "Mission Trading Company." At first the new company, as its name implies, dealt only with trade. Industrial affairs continued under the Industrial Commission of the Mission Committee until 1882, when they were absorbed by the Trading Company upon suggestions from India. This was especially logical because virtually the same people were sitting on both boards. General mission offerings could not be used for commercial enterprises. But capital was needed. Now shares in the company were sold bearing 6 per cent interest. The mission board participated only by investing part of a legacy, 30,000 francs. As time went on some shareholders gave or bequeathed other shares.[8]

There was, however, a closely interlocking directorate between the mission board and the new mission trading company; for the old industrial commission, a subcommittee of the board, directed the new enterprise. President of the company was Ulrich Zellweger, the energetic and clearheaded Swiss banker who had dreamed up the whole idea of a mission trading company, set up its statutes, and persuaded a reluctant, head-shaking mission board to accept it.[9]

The company was organized with 100 shares at 2000 francs each. The shareholders were to receive 6 per cent interest from the profits. Any remaining profit was to be divided equally between the shareholders and the mission. However, any loss was to be borne by the shareholders alone.[10]

At its first organization in 1859, the frankly experimental character of this commercial approach to missions was recognized. The Basel Mission Trading Society was organized for a ten-year trial period. But the visible blessing which rested on its work made its continuance a matter of course. Upon its reorganization in 1869 for a second trial run of an additional decade with capital trebled by the selling of 200 additional shares, the purpose of the Basel Mission Trading Company was stated in these words:

> to promote the work of the Basel Evangelical Mission Society
> by supplying its stations and workshops with needed European

provisions, by introducing the converted Christians and heathen to Christian commerce, and, insofar as God gives his blessing, through financial support.[11]

In the second decade, the basic interest for shareholders was 5 per cent plus half of the annual profits, the mission receiving the other half.[12] However, extra dividends in all but the first year brought the average return to shareholders to 6.65 per cent plus half of the remaining profits.[13]

Like the Christian Brothers much later in California, their "separated brethren" in Basel felt that their commercial venture in missions should get special tax treatment because its income was devoted to sacred purposes. But like the Christian Brothers they were told that the purpose for which they used the income did not change the taxable nature of an enterprise. In a decision in 1879, *Regierungsrat* Niklaus Halter declared that since the Mission Trading Society was "a 'shareholders' corporation organized for commercial profit, for gain within the sense of the law" it would have to pay taxes.[14]

By 1880 the enterprise was in a very strong financial position. In its first two decades there had not been a single year in which shareholders had not received their statutory interest or better plus their proportionate share of half of the remaining profits. But Eduard Preiswerk (1829-1895), successor of Zellweger as leader of the Trading Company, did not want to perpetuate a situation in which shareholders appeared to be profiting from the devotion of missionary merchants who were courting death and disease without salary on modest subsistence allowances. The missionaries themselves did not want this to go on any longer than absolutely necessary, and had often told him so.[15] Now he could rejoice that he was in a position to achieve the aim he had consistently followed for seventeen years, namely to let *all* the surplus profits go to the mission.[16]

But Preiswerk was not ready to take the step of having the mission become the sole shareholder. He feared that the credit of the Trading Company would be jeopardized by the well-known fiscal deficits of the mission. He also thought it best to maintain a separation between mission and trading company against the possibility of persecution in the future.[17] These are the reasons why Preiswerk did not follow the example of C. Kersten & Co., in which case the Unitas Fratrum was the sole shareholder.

Notwithstanding his concern to let the mission get the full profits of the enterprise in the future, Preiswerk was extremely conscientious about giving the shareholders everything that was coming to them under the old statutes. Not only the profits but also the cash reserves of the company were divided between shareholders and mission at the end of the second decade. He was persuaded that the Lord's blessing would rest only on complete integrity according to both the letter and the spirit of the statutes.[18]

The Trading Company was no longer a speculative investment at the end of its second trial decade. Now that it had the legal opportunity to reorganize on a permanent basis, Preiswerk urged the mission to agree to an arrangement whereby the shareholders would receive interest of 5 per cent on a basis so assured "that even anxious souls would regard their participation as a solid investment."[19] The Mission Society owned 120 shares out of 300. And these it was not allowed to sell.[20]

To do justice to the interests of the shareholders, and give them their fair share of the accumulated reserves, they were bought out by increasing the value of each share from 2000 francs to 2500 francs. Hereafter they would receive 5 per cent interest but nothing more. Their shares had, for all practical purposes, become bonds. Of the profits 20 per cent was used as working capital, the rest flowed into the mission treasury. In 1880 the Mission Trading Company was renewed for another twenty years. It was clear that it was organized for the benefit of the mission. As in the previous statutes, those of 1880 called for close supervision by the mission board, which also chose the members of the board of the Trading Company and appointed them to their individual offices.[21] In most cases mission board members were named to key positions in the administration of the Trading Company.

In 1887 the control of the Trading Company by the mission board showed the first signs of loosening. In that year the statutes were revised to provide for an annual shareholders' meeting. Though the mission owned 40 per cent of the shares, it was to be allowed only 20 per cent of the votes represented at any meeting. [22] Henceforth the mission board was allowed to elect only two of the members of the Trading Company's board of directors (Handlungs-Kommission), the other three or four were chosen by the annual shareholders' meeting.[23] As in the statutes of 1880, the ordinary shares were to be secured first in case of loss, while the Mission

Society shares would get only what was left.[24] In the revisions of 1912 the capital was doubled and the Mission Society's proportion of the shares dropped from 40 per cent to 20 per cent, which was all the voting strength it had been allowed under Swiss corporate law since 1887.[25]

The mission trading activities provided very substantial income for the mission treasury. When the Trading Company celebrated its fiftieth anniversary in 1909, it contributed out of the annual profits 354,760 francs to the mission treasury plus a special jubilee gift of 150,000 francs for the pension fund, from which retired or invalid missionaries and widows were supported.[26]

The fifteen shares at 2000 francs each, which the Mission Society purchased with funds from the Christoph Merian legacy in 1859, had increased almost entirely through dividends to 120 shares valued at 2500 francs each. Thus, a 30,000 franc investment had grown to 300,000 francs. Quite aside from dividends on these shares, the Basel Mission Society received a minimum of 15,000,000 francs from the Trading Company during the century from 1859 to 1959. Profits were invested in Christian work overseas as well as in Europe.

The benefits to the mission treasury reached their highest point in the years before World War I as the following table shows:

Contribution to Mission

1870 - 1879	111,000 francs
1880 - 1889	650,000 francs
1890 - 1899	2,020,000 francs
1900 - 1909	2,818,530 francs
1910 - 1913	1,841,834 francs[27]

For 1861 the Mission Society's share of the profits was 18,000 francs.[28] Half a century later, in 1913, on the eve of World War I, contributions to the mission reached their all-time peak with a figure of 1,199,989.67 francs.[29] The actual fiscal contributions were considerably higher than the official figures. Christian love is inventive in finding ways to help. Even so, the financial contributions were not so important as other values received by the Mission Society. We have referred elsewhere to the Christian witness given by industrial and trading personnel, the pedagogic value of work for people unaccustomed to it, the importance of an economic basis for their livelihood and for their contributions to the church. And all along, missionaries got their needed supplies on time and at a reasonable cost.

Sometimes the Trading Company paved the way for the establishment of mission stations. It was able to use its economic leverage at times to persuade African chieftains to keep the peace, thus creating the prerequisites for the coming of a missionary. Sometimes, too, when the Mission Society could not afford to open a mission station, the company could open a trading post, where its *Missionskaufmann* would witness to the gospel.[30]

XV

Separation of the Basel Mission Trading Company from the Mission Society

It was not long before the tension between mission and business made itself felt. Ulrich Zellweger, first head of the Trading Company, was an enterprising merchant, a fast and restless worker, full of big plans for expanding the new company. He wanted to conquer slavery on the Gold Coast through the rapid creation of a whole chain of trading posts and the large-scale promotion of cotton culture. He also wanted to expand commercial operations by engaging mercantile employees independent of the mission at higher compensation than that received by the missionaries.[1] Even an inspector as sympathetic to the place of business in missions as Joseph Josenhans insisted that missions should not be crowded out by commerce, but that business activities must serve the mission and therefore must be willing to develop step by step in a servant role. To Zellweger, this was tieing a ball and chain on a man ready and able to travel with seven-league boots. Finally the tension reached such a pitch that Zellweger resigned in 1864.[2]

Exactly two decades later, the tension between mission and commercial activities provoked another crisis. But this time it was articulated by the other side. The successor to Joseph Josenhans in 1879 was Inspector Otto Schott (1831-1901), a pastor who had been theological instructor in the mission school. He demanded the complete severance of all ties between the mission on the one hand

and industry and trade on the other. The word "mission" was to be removed from the name of all business firms in India, Africa, and Basel.[3] As Zellweger desired independence in the interest of business, so Schott insisted on it in the interest of missions. For him this had become a matter of conscience, and therefore he offered his resignation on January 3, 1884.[4]

The mission board did not want to lose his services. It also made inquiries on the mission field, especially in India.[5] But it was not prepared to accept his demand for the secularization of industry and trade. Particularly did it refuse Schott's ultimatum to take away the honored name "missionary" from the men serving in industry and trade:

> Here we had to say, that we would no longer get the right people for the work; yes, we would soon lose our best and most pious workers, who are in no sense inferior in attitude and mission activity to any ordained missionary, *but who were not sent out as ordinary traders or factory managers, but as missionaries, and have done nothing to deserve being robbed of this title.*[6]

The chairman of the mission board, Professor Riggenbach, emphasized, "This was what all the board members, theologians as well as laymen, could not accept." And therefore, almost half a year after Schott had first offered his resignation, the mission board reluctantly saw itself forced to accept it.[7]

The board reviewed the many advantages of the close connection between mission and business. One telling argument pointed to the mission woodworking and mechanical workshops where African builders were trained. They reminded their supporters: "In Africa every missionary dwelling used to cost a human life because the missionary had to over-exert himself."[8] They were not prepared to say that trade and industry should be part of the mission for all time, but they were unanimous in rejecting Schott's basic demand.[9]

Without mentioning Zellweger by name, the board members referred to the ambitious plans proposed twenty years earlier by "an energetic friend of missions" to send out highly paid employees independent of the mission. But the board was troubled about the position these would occupy alongside the modestly supported missionaries. It concluded that it was not enough for the agents of the Mission Trading Company to be good business people. Above all, they needed to be good Christians, who would be content in the service of the mission with a modest salary.[10] The committee was persuaded that the existing arrangements between mission and economic activities were beneficial and advantageous and that God was blessing them.[11] But as one fruit of the conflict, the committee promised to be all the more zealous to remove anything in the economic activities that would contradict the missionary purpose.[12]

Within twenty-five years, however, the difference in salary level between ordained missionary and Trading Company employee against which the Basel leaders had fought so long was quietly introduced. By the first decade of the twentieth century, workers were no longer being sent out as missionaries with a call to lifetime service, but as employees under a limited contract at a salary higher than that ordained missionaries received. The work, especially in Africa, was no longer being expanded at a rate dependent on the availability of consecrated missionary personnel. Now business opportunity dictated expansion. Salary was governed by supply and demand in the labor market.[13]

However, the Basel Mission Trading Company did try to sustain a wholesome attitude toward the mission work and purpose in its new employees by calling G. Josenhans, former general president of the Basel Mission on the Gold Coast, to be head of personnel and to maintain a personal relationship with the young people in its expanding work.[14]

The Trading Company increased its working capital by doubling the number of shares. Then it doubled its capital again by a large loan from a banking consortium.[15] On the eve of World War I, the company was, however, not only vastly larger than the infant company of fifty years earlier, but was also different in spirit. It was following the dynamics of business expansion. The dreams of Ulrich Zellweger were being achieved. No longer were Trading Company workers on the same level as missionaries in call and conditions of work.[16] One of the basic issues over which Schott resigned had been removed.

In 1912 C. Pfleiderer, on behalf of the Trading Company, reviewed the history of the organization for the many new shareholders. He pointed to its aims of promoting missions in social, spiritual, and material ways. He told them that the Trading Company wanted only

to be a valued serving maid in the work of the Kingdom of
God, and that the mission administration in Basel had never
been able to share the opinion that only that is a truly spiritual
mission, where nothing but the office of preaching is carried
out; for he is spiritual who is filled with the Spirit of God in
any branch of the work of God.[17]

It took World War I to accomplish the complete organizational
separation of the Trading Company from the mission. Over half the
missionaries and mission offerings as well as home base staff
members came from Germany.[18] One can understand, therefore,
why many circles mistakenly regarded both the Basel Mission
Society and the Trading Company as German, even though both
were legally Swiss corporations. Moreover, the popular mind had
long erroneously regarded the Mission Society and the Mission
Trading Company as a single entity because they shared a common
aim.[19]

In an endeavor to placate the British, the mission disposed of all
its shares in the Trading Company in 1917. None of the profits were
to go to the support of mission societies from countries at war with
Great Britain or its allies. No longer was any of the profit to flow
into the Basel Mission Society treasury. Wilhelm Preiswerk-Imhoff,
head of the Trading Company, gave up his membership on the board
of the Mission Society.[20]

Now the object of the company was revised to read: "Trade in
Europe and with overseas areas as well as every activity connected
therewith in mercantile, craft and industrial matters." And the
benevolent clause was changed to read: "Furtherance of evangelical
endeavors for the spreading of the Kingdom of God."[21] A
committee of three to five native Swiss were to administer the
distribution of surplus profits according to this provision.[22] And in
1928 the word "Mission" was dropped at the request of the Mission
Society;[23] the firm has been known ever since as the Basel Trading
Company Ltd.

At present, the company pays its shareholders a maximum of 6
per cent. The remainder of the distributable profits is allocated every
year, through the medium of a committee of administrators, to
projects furthering evangelical endeavors. In exceptional cases, purely
philanthropic work may also be supported.[24] Though it no longer
carries "Mission" in its name, no one can say that the Basel Trading

Company has been completely secularized. It still makes contributions to the furtherance of the Kingdom of God.

The greatest difficulties and crises of the company's century-long
history, just as in the case of the Jesuits in Paraguay or Zeisberger
among the Indians, came not from heathen obduracy but from
nominal fellow Christians and the governments of so-called Christian
lands. World War I showed the world the disgraceful spectacle of
Europe's "Christian" nations slaughtering a whole generation of
their youth. This turned the respect of Asia and Africa to horrified
disgust. The Christian world mission has not yet recovered from the
shock, particularly since the added devastation of World War II and
the first use of the atomic bomb against an Asian people by
America, a nation supposedly less tainted than the older reprobates
of Europe.

It was a Christian nation, Great Britain, the very country for
which Elias Schrenk helped save the Gold Coast, that confiscated all
the properties of the Basel Mission Trading Company in World War I,
even though it was a Swiss corporation. In his detailed history of the
company, Wanner devotes 125 pages to the company's struggle to
recover its property.[25] The men of Basel had always appreciated the
liberal spirit of the British colonial administration and the freedom it
gave them for maximum service to the people of India and Africa.
All the greater their indignation at seeing themselves stripped of
their properties—in the Camerouns already at the beginning of the
War, on the Gold Coast at the end, and in India six months after the
Armistice. This was due to war psychosis, misunderstandings, and
the fact that at the outbreak of the war the Trading Company had
many Germans on its staff and a number of Germans as shareholders—approximately 13 per cent.

In both the Camerouns the Basel Trading Company got back its
small possessions by 1923.[26] The Gold Coast proved far more
difficult. The colonial authorities there had placed the seized
properties under the control of Commonwealth Trust Limited, a
corporation of shareholders who were to receive 5 per cent interest,
while any additional profit was to be devoted to religious and
educational purposes. The colonial secretary had to approve the
administrative officers of the Commonwealth Trust Limited, and he
himself appointed the trustees who were to distribute any profits.[27]

The colonial secretary paid high compliments to the enterprise he was expropriating, whose assets in liquid cash alone amounted to £263,462:[28]

> The Basle Mission Factory—as it was known locally—was an extremely prosperous trading concern. . . . It is obvious, that the Factory, to a substantial extent, did aid missionary work in this Colony and, moreover, it was the only company in the Colony which did not trade in liquor. . . .

He lauded the "high religious tone which has always distinguished the Basel Mission Trading Society" and then expressed the hope that "if the Commonwealth Trust brings to the business anything like the same energy and ability that the Basle Mission Factory did, its profits will be very considerable."[29]

But they could not confiscate the unique Basel spirit which made the enterprise go, a heritage compounded of canny business sense, hard work, Christian missionary dedication, readiness to live for Christ and, if need be, to die for him. The Commonwealth Trust Limited took over the most prosperous business on the Gold Coast, with a large cash balance, but proved unable to manage this going concern with profit. However, in extenuation, it must be pointed out that those were years in which many other Gold Coast enterprises suffered losses.[30]

What was the role played by Christian leaders of ecumenical missionary circles in the problem of the Basel Mission Trading Company properties? This has been the subject of much misunderstanding and criticism, especially on the part of German mission supporters. All German properties in Allied countries and possessions were to be confiscated for the payment of German debts to citizens of Allied countries, according to the provisions of the Versailles Treaty signed on June 28, 1919. These general terms would have spelled a dissolution of the German mission societies. However, due mainly to the efforts of J. H. Oldham,[31] who had emerged as an outstanding ecumenical leader in his preparatory role for the World Missionary Conference at Edinburgh in 1910, a provision—Article 438—was included in the Versailles Treaty which stipulated that the property of German missions, "including that of trading societies whose profits were devoted to the support of missions shall continue to be devoted to missionary purposes."[32]

The inclusion of trading societies in this provision is significant. Though not the only mission trading society, Basel was the largest and best known. It is difficult to avoid the conclusion that this provision referred primarily to Basel, which because of its large number of German workers and shareholders was erroneously but somewhat understandably regarded as a German operation. But these shareholders were bought out by Swiss citizens. And the British government interned or removed from the field the German missionaries, including those affiliated with Basel.

The Versailles Treaty led to fury and bitterness in Germany, and in large part to World War II. For this reason it was difficult for German missionary leaders to assess even Article 438 objectively. As they viewed the situation, John R. Mott and J. H. Oldham had silently stood by while their societies were despoiled. This only compounded their distrust of these two men. Few could rise above the warping hatreds of war to realize that Article 438 had actually saved their mission properties. As it turned out, these were restored to them.

Strangely, the Basel Mission Trading Society, even though legally not a German but a Swiss organization, had a much harder time getting back its properties than any of the ordinary mission operations that were legally German. Ironically, it was the well-meant efforts of British missionary leaders to save the properties from sale as enemy possessions that made it so difficult for the rightful owners to get back what was theirs. Article 438 required that the property of "trading societies whose profits were devoted to the support of missions, shall continue to be devoted to missionary purposes." Such properties were to be administered by boards of trustees. Oldham himself had suggested the trustee system, as he declared in Basel in November, 1919. He felt he deserved praise rather than blame for it.[33]

But the Basel Mission Trading Company properties on the Gold Coast were sequestered long before Article 438 was adopted in 1919 with the rest of the Versailles Treaty. Already on January 31, 1918, the Secretary of State for the Colonies in London instructed the Legislative Council of the Gold Coast to deport all remaining European members of the Basel Mission Society and the Basel Mission Trading Company. Soon thereafter in 1918 the Legislative Council of the Gold Coast passed emergency legislation paving the way to seize and sell at auction the properties of the Basel Mission Trading Company.[34]

To head off this sale, representatives of British missionary circles sped into action, wanting this valuable business to continue to benefit the mission cause. They were joined by representatives of philanthropic bodies, who were much attracted by the fact that the Trading Company had refrained from selling liquor. They thought it a pity that the operation should fall into hands that could not be expected to preserve this tradition. Together they were able to persuade the British government that the Basel Mission Trading Company properties in Ghana should not be treated as ordinary enemy property but should be retained and administered by some approved purchaser on the lines previously followed by the Swiss owners. The Secretary of State for the Colonies, Mr. (later Lord) Walter Long, dispatched a telegram on December 3, 1918, in consequence of which the property was vested in trustees.[35]

During 1918, attempts were made by British missionary and philanthropic leaders to form a private syndicate that would purchase the Trading Society's properties; however, they could not raise the necessary money. At this point a misunderstanding arose that was to have fateful consequences. The conclusion was reached that the property might be regarded as impressed with a trust for the benefit of the native population. It was decided that the assets could therefore be transferred to trustees without any further compensation to the original owners than the return of their nominal capital of £120,000. The plan was, accordingly, adopted to form a small company for the purpose of carrying on the business and administering the existing assets of the Trading Society.[36]

The Basel Mission Trading Company denied emphatically that it was a trust,[37] insisting that a private company consisting of shareholders could not be a trust.[38] It maintained that the generous help it had given to the Basel Mission in the past was done at the free will of the Trading Company in accordance with statutes which it was at liberty to change at any time. That this view was essentially correct is proved by the fact that the Trading Company had drastically altered its statutes in 1917. All references to support of the Basel Mission Society were stricken. Now the statutes included the categorical statement: "Any support of societies whose leaders are citizens of countries with which Great Britain and its Allies are at war is out of the question."[39]

However, this was not understood at first in Britain either by missionary or government circles. And thus the Commonwealth Trust Ltd. came into being. Kenneth Maclennan played a leading role in the new corporation. He was a man of many parts. After serving for a number of years as a missionary in India, he returned to Scotland to serve with the Laymen's Missionary Movement. As Associate Secretary of the World Missionary Conference at Edinburgh in 1910, he became a close co-worker of J. H. Oldham, who was Secretary. Together they served as secretaries of the Continuation Committee after Edinburgh, of the Standing Committee of the Conference of British Missionary Societies, and of the Emergency Committee of Cooperating Missions. In addition, during the war years as "gun contractor" in the munitions ministry, Maclennan was responsible for providing all artillery supplies to the British Army. He was regarded as a very able administrator.

Wilhelm Preiswerk-Imhoff, head of the Basel Mission Trading Company, journeyed to London with his eldest son in March 1919 to protest the confiscation of the company properties. But they failed completely in their endeavors to persuade the Commonwealth Trust Ltd. Particularly Maclennan, a director of the Trust, proved impervious to every argument.[40]

Failing to secure any help for their cause in British missionary circles, Preiswerk and his son turned to men in politics. This was in every way the right move, for it was the government and not the missionary and philanthropic groups that had committed the injustice of confiscating a neutral concern. The man who proved of particular help was Viscount Templetown (1853-1939), a member of the House of Lords. To Preiswerk, who met him for the first time in 1923, Viscount Templetown was the embodiment of the British gentleman, who stands for justice and fair play. Viscount Templetown took the matter up in Parliament. The case was debated in both houses. Hermann Rottmann's little trading post on the Gold Coast and the small beginnings in India had become *that* important. Viscount Templetown said forthrightly: "I want to see the name of England cleared of this scandal which has been going on for ten years."[41] He found much support. The Earl of Selborne, for example, appealed to "remove this discredit from England."[42]

After a long and bitter struggle, Swiss pertinacity and British fairness finally triumphed. The Basel Trading Company once more gained possession of its properties on the Gold Coast in the fall of 1928. This made it possible to expand the activities of the Union Trading Company, which the Basel Trading Company had formed already in 1921 to make a fresh start on the Gold Coast.

The Basel Trading Company was reimbursed to the extent of £250,000 cash plus the return of its buildings on the Gold Coast. The Commonwealth Trust Ltd. was to receive the supplies on hand in the buildings plus £55,000 to enable them to acquire other quarters.[43] These monies had to be paid out of the funds of the Gold Coast. But this was not unjust, for it was the Gold Coast Legislative Council that had taken the initiative in wrongly confiscating the properties of the Basel Mission Trading Company in the first place. Moreover, the Colony would now have the benefit of two companies devoting a portion of their income to the spiritual and social welfare of the people.[44]

The people of the Gold Coast had gotten nothing out of the Commonwealth Trust Limited. Embarrassing questions in the house of Commons elicited the information that no surplus profits had been earned by the Commonwealth Trust Ltd. in the first nine years of its existence and no payments had therefore been made to the trustees for the purposes of education in the Gold Coast.[45] Not only that, dividends were five years in arrears.

Of course, the situation looked altogether different from the standpoint of the Commonwealth Trust. It had assumed responsibility at a time when the bottom dropped out of the cocoa market. The price fell from 126 shillings a cwt. in February 1920 to 37 shillings before the end of the year. Large and well-established concerns on the Gold Coast showed enormous losses and a number went bankrupt. The company's losses were formidable but it held on until economic conditions gradually improved.[46]

When the Basel Trading Company got back its old properties, the British government expressly made the condition "that in the future as in the past they will not sell spirituous liquor, guns, arms or gunpowder to natives."[47] A further condition was

> that they will adhere to their established practice of devoting a substantial proportion of their distributable profits to missionary and other philanthropic purposes in all parts of the world including the British Empire [through the medium of trustees] and that in the application of such proportion full regard will be paid to the needs of the Gold Coast Colony on a scale not less than has been followed in the past.[48]

CONFISCATION IN INDIA

The same war psychosis that prevailed on the Gold Coast

prompted the seizure of the Basel Mission Trading Company properties in India. The transfer to the Commonwealth Trust Limited did not, however, take place until 26 January, 1920, more than two weeks after the Versailles Treaty had gone into effect (10 January, 1920).

Just as in Africa, the Commonwealth Trust Limited proved a failure in commercial management. Persistent questioners in the House of Commons learned that the once prosperous Basel enterprises in India had not made one rupee of distributable profits up to 1928.[49]

Meanwhile, how was the Basel Trading Company faring during these same difficult 1920's? Though it had been unjustly stripped of its properties in Africa and India, it managed to stay in business. Its credit was still good. It borrowed a million francs in 1923 at 6 per cent. Ironically, the company contributed substantial amounts to "the furtherance of evangelical endeavors for the spreading of the Kingdom of God" in obedience to its statutes and its long tradition during the very years when the Commonwealth Trust Ltd. was unable to do so, in spite of the fact that it had the properties! Of course, Basel had certain important advantages over the Trust— experienced leadership and staff, and a clear, unassailed title to the business it was operating.

Contributions of the Basel Trading Company
During the 1920's

1923	Fr. 215,000
1925	180,000
1926	180,000
1927	240,000[50]

It should be noted, however, that as time went on the contribution record of the Commonwealth Trust Ltd. was to improve markedly. By 1961 it could look back on total grants of £58,458 to missionary, welfare, and education projects in Ghana,[51] while the corresponding sum for India reached £61,635.[52]

Six years after the restitution of the African properties, justice was still delayed in India. Lord Templetown, the unwearied champion of British conscience, was magnificent in an eloquent speech to the House of Lords in 1934: "There seems to be a flouting, nothing less, of Magna Carta. What does Magna Carta say? It says very distinctly: 'To no one will we refuse justice or delay right or justice.' Now justice delayed is justice denied. I have been at this question for ten years. . . . However, I hope that some day I shall see daylight."[53]

But Lord Templetown did not live to see the case concluded. The assets confiscated in India were valued at £379,380 in 1920. By 1950 at 5 per cent interest the loss stood at £968,716. In 1952, thirty-three years after confiscation, the Basel Trading Company, with the approval of the House of Commons, accepted a settlement of all its claims in India in the amount of £125,000 plus £1,050 for legal costs incurred.[54]

In 1928, however, after war hysteria had died down somewhat, the Secretary of State for the Colonies, L. S. Amery, had declared forthrightly:

> I took the best legal opinion available to me and was advised that the action taken in 1918 had in fact amounted to seizing without compensation the property and buildings of citizens of a neutral state, and it was therefore impossible to justify in a legal action or arbitration regarding it as a war measure on the ground of the enemy association of the former owners.[55]

Why did the Commonwealth Trust Ltd., however, resist suggestions to return its properties to the Basel Trading Company after the British government admitted that they had been unjustly seized? This question troubled the Reverend Frank Short, secretary of the Conference of Mission Societies in Great Britain and Ireland, and a trustee of the Commonwealth Education and Welfare Trust, which dispenses profits entrusted to it by the Commonwealth Trust Ltd. After a careful examination of about twenty years of the correspondence and public discussion of the issue, Short concludes that J. H. Oldham realized too late that the seizure of the Basel Trading Company's properties was mistaken. But by the time he had reached this understanding the new company had been formed, and Oldham felt he could not accept as satisfactory any solution which removed one act of injustice by creating another.[56]

Unjust confiscation had been the act of government in the Gold Coast and in India.[57] It had not been the act of the Commonwealth Trust Ltd. Why should the Trust alone bear the cost of redressing that injustice?[58] Lord Carson declared in the House of Lords that this would amount to saying to the public-spirited directors and shareholders of the Commonwealth Trust Ltd.: "True it is, the

Colonial Office says, we formed you in 1918, and you took over this for us: it was very good of you, but we now tell you to turn out and hand over these assets."[59]

Even Viscount Templetown, while he fought like a lion for the rights of the Basel Trading Company, never did it at the expense of the Commonwealth Trust Ltd. In one of his finest statements, he declares: "I would defy anybody to find a single word that I ever said against the Commonwealth Trust, or against their claim for justice. I have asked for justice for the Basel Mission Trading Company, and therefore I was perfectly willing to yield it to the Commonwealth Trust."[60] And the Lord Bishop of Southwark must have been speaking for many when he stated:

> I hope the noble Lord who will reply to this debate will be able to tell us that the Government appreciates the public-spirited action which was taken by those who formed this Trust and that they will see that opportunity is given for the continuance of its work.[61]

That careful and remarkably objective student of this unhappy history, Frank Short, regards it as sheer tragedy that J. H. Oldham and Wilhelm Preiswerk-Imhoff, the president of the Basel Mission Trading Company at the time of World War I, did not meet before the decision was taken to create the Commonwealth Trust. Short feels this would have had two salutory effects: 1) The relationship between the Trading Company and the Mission would have become clear. 2) Oldham would have understood that the company was not impressed with a trust but freely chose to devote its profits to philanthropic and religious uses.

For the Basel Trading Company the issue was different. Because of its German associations, the Basel Mission Society had been forced by the government to cease operations in British territory. Therefore the Basel Trading Company had to establish the reality of its constitutional freedom both in what it did with its distributable profits and in its association with the Basel Mission Society.[62]

The whole episode underlines the tragedy of World War I, which pitted Christians against their brothers and put a mournful end to what had been the "great century" in missions. In spite of the World Missionary Conference at Edinburgh in 1910, which had brought new unity to Christians, once the war broke out, many were guided more by national passions than by feelings of identity with

Christians in enemy countries.[63] The Swiss and German leaders and supporters of the Basel Mission Society at home maintained their unity unbroken through the war years, but only at the cost of losing their mission fields in Africa and India, and all their properties. This attitude also caused the Basel Mission Trading Company to lose its possessions in India and Africa.[64]

The effort to maintain the unity of Swiss and German in the Mission Society made it all the more imperative for the Trading Society to separate itself from the former. Here their interests sharply diverged. If confronted with the painful choice between German co-workers and the Trading Society, the Mission Society almost inevitably had to choose the former, not only because of century-old ties of joint work, but also because the Germans were even more vital to its life than the Trading Society. Over half of the Society's contributions and by far the greater portion of its missionaries came from Germany. But as the political lines in World War I were drawn, these same German associations struck at the very life of the Trading Company. The ecumenical association that is highly desirable for the communion of saints in missions, was in this instance fearfully dangerous to an economic enterprise. Nevertheless, the Basel Trading Company still devotes a portion of its distributable profits to the Kingdom of God through a variety of ecclesiastical, missionary, educational, and charitable causes both overseas and at home.[65] Through the Union Trading Company, its affiliate in Africa, the Basel Trading Company devotes substantial sums to technical training and scholarships. It supports a number of schools for vocational training.

The Basel Trading Society in some ways resembles a foundation; however, unlike most foundations it not only invests money but engages in direct commercial activity. And for Christians, this is in some important ways preferable. Money is impersonal, but living people are required to carry on a business. The Basel Trading Company has always sought to send out high-quality Christians to make their witness in the market place. They have not hid their light under a bushel of stock certificates; they set it high upon the candlestick of a living demonstration of the gospel in the factory and across the counter.

In its history, organization, and purpose, the Basel Trading Company may still have something to say to Christian businessmen today. This is a further reason why I have devoted so much space to

this effort. There is great need for capital and skill and Christian
character in the lands across the sea, in the inner city, in rural
pockets of poverty in the West. Over more than a century, the men
of Basel have worked out many of the problems inherent in using
economic activities for mission.

Today the Basel Trading Company is more active than ever on the
west coast of Africa, through its affiliate, the Union Trading Co.
Ltd. It operates a kaleidoscopic variety of business enterprises in
Ghana, Nigeria, Cameroun, and Liberia. In Accra, it owns one of the
best department stores on the whole west coast of Africa, a large
five-story structure. No longer is it connected in the popular mind
with the Basel Mission Society, but especially under the name of the
Union Trading Company it is well and favorably known throughout
this area for the Christian character of its personnel, and for offering
"quality goods at reasonable prices," its long-time slogan. Among
missionaries it is also appreciated for its helpfulness in supplying
their needs.[66]

In India, where the Basel Mission Trading Company lost its
industries, the Mission Society still cherishes its tradition of
industrial missions, but expresses it now through vocational training
efforts. This may be a more appropriate avenue in the India of
today, in which employer-employee relations have become so
difficult and so delicate, especially for Westerners. Some years ago
the Mission Society was happy to see the opening of a Technical
Training School in Nettur on the west coast of India. It was initiated
at the suggestion of the Society by the *Hilfswerk der Evangelischen
Kirchen der Schweiz* (HEKS) to combat unemployment. Unlike the
older factories of the Basel Mission Trading Company, this institution is intended for training rather than production. Soon, a second
training center was established at Dharwar. Now a production center
has been opened in Katpadi near Madras with the purpose of
providing practical experience on a broader scale to the persons
trained at Nettur and Dharwar. It also has the additional purpose of
meeting, in part, the costs of the training institutions. The training
and production centers have been formed into a foundation closely
connected with the Church of South India. With the help of *Brot für
die Welt,* the Basel Mission Society itself established a training center
on the premises of the Basel Mission Press in Mangalore. When the
program is under way, it will train fifty apprentices in simple tool
making. Indian, Swiss, and German engineers are in charge of this

project, called Hebich Technical Training School in honor of one of the first Basel missionaries in Mangalore, Samuel Hebich. Early in 1964 a carpenter was sent out to provide training in wood-working and cabinetmaking at an orphanage started by the Basel Mission and now conducted by the Church of South India.

The spirit of Basel lives on.

XVI

Balance Sheet on the Basel
Mission Trading Company

Attacks aimed at the very life of the Basel Mission Trading Company came not only from without but also from within. The gravest confrontation took place when Otto Schott resigned as executive head of the Basel Mission Society in protest against economic activities. This sharp encounter yields most of the criticisms—and rejoinders—which we rehearse in this chapter.

1) *Criticism:* The industries keep the people dependent on the mission as their factory boss.

Answer: In Africa it was relatively easy to make the people economically independent; in India it is much harder. Many peasants are independent in name only; in fact, landlords oppress them and moneylenders suck their blood. A job in the Basel industries is actually their economic and spiritual salvation.[1]

2) *Criticism:* In starting new plants, commercial interests can easily take precedence over mission concerns.

Answer: Regrettably, this has happened in one instance, and the board will do its best to strengthen the missionary effectiveness of this plant.[2]

3) *Criticism:* Too many heathen are employed.

Answer: Many of them become Christians. (Half a century later, after most of the workmen were Christians, the critique was reversed to demand a larger portion of non-Christians—the way it had been in the first place.) A sizeable proportion of hard-working non-Christian employees would be healthy competition for complacent Christians who entertain the unwarranted expectation "that Christians as Christians, however inefficient they may be and however uneconomic the activity in which they are employed, have a right to demand work in Christian industries and businesses."[3]

4) *Criticism:* Non-Christians are "forced" to attend the fifteen-minute factory devotions at the beginning of the working day.

Answer: This criticism would apply far more to mission schools, in which non-Christian pupils are required to attend Christian religious instruction as well as devotions. It would apply to many schools in the sending countries.[4]

5) *Criticism:* The desire for employment in the mission industries is tainting the validity of some conversions.

Answer: Theodore Oehler, head of the Basel Mission after Schott resigned, made this able defense: "The end which we aim at in our industrial enterprise is not to rouse in the heathen the desire of being converted. We only aim at making it possible for those who have this desire to carry it out." He pointed out that the tileries, with their hard work, considered degrading by Hindus, with their strict discipline, and with their modest wages, had very few attractions for the converts, many of whom had been in comfortable circumstances before their conversion.

6) *Criticism:* Many attempts at industrial missions by ordained missionaries have failed in India.

Answer: What else could be expected? Inadequate capital, lack of technical and business training, want of experience and of continuity as long as the matter was left up to the occasional taste or aptitude of an ordained missionary easily explained such failures.[5]

7) *Criticism:* Why are employees in Basel mission industries paid more than the average Indian earns? Is this indulging the idleness of Christian converts and their more expensive mode of life?

Answer: The Christian life costs more. Missionaries expect Christians to go to church on Sunday decently dressed, to pay school fees for their children, to buy a few books, and so on. Since the mission expects all these things from them, and furthermore appeals to their Christian liberality on many occasions, the mission industries cannot well ignore this in valuing the work of a diligent Christian workman. Besides, in most cases the wages of a non-Christian laborer are only part of his income. A Christian has nothing but his wages. He has lost his former relatives and his share of the family property.[6]

8) *Criticism:* The Basel mission industries are destroying indigenous weaving methods and craftsmanship.

Answer: "If our cloth has a good sale and the European loom is better than the Indian, I think the sympathy with what is national is carried too far if we are asked to persuade our people to dig a hole in the ground, use the Indian loom, make saris, and starve."[7]

However, though there was no lack of criticism, a great many positive evaluations of mission industries and commerce were also expressed. In general, the Basel economic activities helped the Basel Mission reduce the discouraging membership losses suffered by many missions whose converts were driven in their search for a livelihood to move to other parts, where they often were lost to the Christian church.

It must be emphasized again that the Basel industries were not something apart from the missionary functions, but an integral piece of Christian nurture and witness. The European superintendent considered the Christian development of his workers a part of his responsibility. Making more and better Christians and making more and better tiles were all part of the same day's work.

When the Arakallu branch was established, Christian workmen from Jeppoo were selected with special care because of the witness they could make to the surrounding non-Christian environment. This workshop became a valuable mission medium. Many unemployed catechumens were supported—and tested—through their work in the tile factory.[8]

An English visitor to the tile work in 1881 said: "These Germans are hard-working people and they also know how to get others to work; in all of India it is well known: what the Germans do, they do thoroughly, and therefore their products are in such demand." The hard-working, faithful Swiss and German missionary tilers were appreciated by the non-Christians as well. The first superintendent of the Arakallu tile works, Feuchter of Württemberg, was held in such reverence by the people that they regarded him as a sanyassin—until he got married.

The willingness to employ non-Christians helped relieve the mission industry approach of the opprobrium of tainted conversions. As a matter of fact, there has been far more danger of rice Christians in the more conventional missions. Without industrial establishments, they often employed a large proportion of their converts as servants, loaned them funds, or simply gave them handouts. On a visit to India in the 1890's, a German pastor who distinguished himself as a keen and critical observer found conditions that sound dishearteningly contemporary. He discovered that some missionaries loaned their workers money at 12 per cent to get them out of the clutches of moneylenders. If they had loaned the money at 6 per cent, the people would have sublet it, since the moneylender's minimum was 15 per cent.

He was also discouraged to find many Christian outcastes calling the missionary "Mabap," that is, "You are my mother and my father." It was difficult for the missionary not to become paternalistic. The German critic vastly preferred the Basel approach:

> Many mission friends at home who regard missions in a one-sided manner as a purely spiritual matter complain about this involvement with worldly things. But if they could see with their own eyes the blessed effects of industry they would surely wish that it would experience a much greater expansion.[9]

A missionary of another denomination came to criticize the Basel weaving industries but left to praise. His prime concern was this: Are the large factory industries proletarianizing the people, making them weak, dependent, and lazy? Or are they helping to develop thrifty, respectable, self-supporting Christians? He found that the latter was decidedly the case. The industrial missionaries dealt with the people according to honest business principles, firm and yet generous. They were concerned with the moral character of their workers and with their presence at devotions, and they encouraged church attendance, though they did not make it mandatory. On top of this, the industries helped many workers acquire their own homes.

But above all, the mission industries impressed this visitor as an object lesson to the community and the world that a large business could be carried out not for the enrichment of any particular individuals, but for the good of mankind and for the extension of the Kingdom of God. He found men well trained in their trades, devoting their energies to a business in which they had no pecuniary interest, and yet making it a commercial success, a thing which a businessman in Madras had told him was an impossibility.[10]

The men of Basel could speak of "Christian commerce," a phrase that would have seemed a contradiction to economically unrealistic philosophers and theologians through the ages. Their early Basel objective of "introducing the converted Christians and heathen to Christian commerce" said much about their faith. They believed that mammon could and should be used for mission. It witnessed to their conviction that Christianity had been a blessing to the physical and commercial life of Europe. They saw themselves as people who had enjoyed great advantages and now had a pedagogic duty to the disadvantaged.

Whenever the topic of industrial missions appeared on the program of outstanding nineteenth-century missionary conferences, the work of the Basel Mission was cited as a shining example. An early instance is the first General Missions Conference at Allahabad, India, in 1872.[11] This assembly also noted with great interest that after the introduction of mission industries, the per capita church offerings of Indian Christians in the Basel Mission had doubled.

However, not only Westerners, but also Africans paid high tribute to the commercial-industrial missionaries of Basel. Hermann L. Rottmann, Gold Coast pioneer *Missionskaufmann,* received this encomium from a native pastor who is remarkable as an early West African historian:

> The Mission Trade Society had begun their operations to prepare the way for the Lord by trade based on Christian principles. The first Factory was established at Christiansborg in 1855 by our energetic missionary merchant, Mr. H. L. Rottmann. We feel compelled to remark here that he has, during a period of 37 years, devoted all his energy in that capacity cf a missionary merchant and has thoroughly convinced many an intelligent and patriotic native by his simplicity, honesty, sobriety and self-denial as a missionary indeed. We say convinced, because the general notion prevalent on the whole Gold Coast is, that a merchant *nolens volens* becomes a worldling, a polygamist and luxurious.[12]

To this day, in fact, the Union Trading Company, the Basel Trading Company affiliate, enjoys the high respect of Africans. They refer to it familiarly as "B.M.F."—"the Black Man's Friend." These letters were the well-known initials of the old Basel Mission Factory (literally, trading post).[13]

And in India, too, the contributions of the Basel industries are remembered with gratitude by nationals. When President Jacques Rossel, chief executive of the Basel Mission Society, visited India, a civic spokesman offered this tribute:

> Almost all of us are indebted to the Basel Mission in one way or another. It may be the education we have had, it may be the leaflets on religion or the books which we possess, or the *banian* we wear or the tiles that cover our roofs that have come to us from the Basel Mission. The Basel Missions were the pioneers in the educational field in our District. . . . The first tile factory, the first printing press, the first hosiery factory, the first mechanical works were the fruits of their labor and our District is not a little indebted to them for all their selfless projects in our midst.[14]

Fulsome addresses are familiar to every official visitor to India. However, it is significant that a civic leader put industrial missions on the same footing with Christian schools and literature as valid mission activities, and that he still gratefully recalled the Basel Mission industries almost half a century after their expropriation.

What of the Basel Mission Society leadership today? How does it feel in retrospect about the much-controverted mission industries? No doubt there are still various opinions. However, President Rossel, while aware of the weaknesses and disadvantages, has come to judge the industries invaluable precisely from the missionary standpoint. He recalls the period from 1926 to 1939, when Dr. Karl Hartenstein, a distinguished theologian and ecumenical leader, was at the helm of the Society. Hartenstein's slogan was "Concentration on essentials!" He was deeply influenced by the early Karl Barth,[15] and his overwhelming emphasis on God's self-disclosure in Jesus Christ, on the Word of God, and on the proclamation of the gospel. This may have been at least in part responsible for Hartenstein's relative lack of sympathy for industrial missions and mission schools. But the upshot today, in the view of Dr. Rossel, is that by this exclusive concentration on the spiritual aspect of the work, the Basel Mission Society in India has lost much of its *Reibungsfläche*—a concept difficult to translate—its "friction-surface," its power to influence and make an impact on the people.[16]

Any evaluation also must take into account that the Basel commercial establishments, especially in India, were virtually the sole financial support of the Basel missionaries and their work during World War I. As late as 1918, the mission could say that it had never lacked money in India, even though support from Basel was cut off by the war.[17]

Why did the men of Basel succeed in exerting such a wholesome mission influence through their commercial endeavors? No doubt, there were many factors. Perhaps we can identify a few of them.

1) They came into undeveloped areas and pioneered what later became state-wide enterprises, such as weaving and tilemaking in India, or the trade and cocoa culture on the west coast of Africa.

2) Like the Moravians, the Basel Mission Society considered the commercial and technical men missionaries, except that they were not ordained. It did not make artisans and merchants second-class citizens in the Christian world mission.

3) The Basel Mission Society trained the lay apostolate for its work of articulating and demonstrating the gospel. Artisans and merchants were trained at the Basel *Missionshaus,* though much more briefly than the missionaries who preached.[18] Hendrik Kraemer has spoken of laymen as the "frozen assets" of the church.[19] There has been much visionary talk about the lay apostolate as the great mission force of the future. Without training such as was given at the Basel *Missionshaus* in earlier times, the vast Antarctica of the lay apostolate is not going to be thawed out.

4) The Basel Mission Society kept the industrial and mercantile workers in one missionary community with the ordained emissaries on the field. It was no easy problem to shape their relation to each other. At first the industrial and mercantile missionaries had been fully subordinated to the ordained missionaries. This often led to friction. Again, sometimes lay brothers reached out for the rights of the ordained. For example, in India a certain brother caused trouble by administering the Lord's Supper and Baptism without license. For about forty years before 1909, the lay brothers enjoyed complete equality with the ordained missionaries in conference membership, salary, etc. At first, however, they had to live from their receipts—in Africa until 1878, in India somewhat earlier. For generations the merchants and industrial technicians carried the honored title of missionary.

5) The Basel Mission was at great pains to emphasize the missionary nature of the task which the industrial and mercantile brothers performed. It made no unbiblical distinction between the

secular and the sacred, the material and the spiritual. It rejected the
critique of those who regarded the mission activities in material
things as not germane to the mission task.[20]

6) The Basel Mission believed that in the interest of spreading the
gospel it had a legitimate cultural service to render the people of
Asia and Africa. It did not regard European products, their
manufacture and sale, as ends in themselves. But these provided
opportunity to demonstrate how a Christian cares for and meets the
needs of his fellow man. Manufactured products and trade goods
gave these down-to-earth missionaries a chance to share with others
the qualities of service, integrity, and joy in productive labor which,
in their best and highest expression, came not from the ethos of
Greece and Rome but were gifts of the New Testament inherited by
much of European culture. As Schlatter declared,

> He who believes in the power and the purpose of the Gospel to
> penetrate the life of men and nations in all their relationships
> and activities, cannot deny to missions the right to trade and
> industry. In this conviction the Basel Mission did its work and
> it was not put to shame.[21]

Why then, in spite of this conviction, did mission and economic
activities come to lose all organizational ties with one another?

It would be oversimplifying to point only to the obvious rupture
brought about by World War I. The reasons are complex. First, there
is the problem of the divergency of aims in missions and economic
activities. Each has its own inner dynamics and seeks to obey its own
laws. The first clear step toward separation seems to have been taken
by the Basel Trading Company about 1909, when it expanded far
more rapidly than the supply of mission-minded workers allowed.
Inspector Schott had resigned in 1884, when this trend first showed
itself. At that time, the mission board had vowed to keep expansion
subservient to missionary purposes.[22]

On the other hand, it is fair to ask whether the Christian churches
of Europe did their very best to motivate and recruit[23] an adequate
number of mission-minded workers for the Trading Company. The
Mission Society published books on the economic ministry for the
obvious purpose of recruitment, appealing particularly to Christian
youth organizations. But evidently the latter could not supply an
adequate number of mission-minded workers for rapidly expanding
opportunities, and very soon it became standard practice to send out

workers under short-term contract at higher salaries than those of the ordained missionaries.[24]

All of which is to say that in terms of ecclesiological structure, the mission society, in spite of its great and historic contributions to the cause of missions, may be inadequate for the role of arbiter when tension arises between missions and ancillary economic activities.

A third reason for the sharp separation that came about between missions and economic activities in Basel is found in an inadequate internationalism. The reader may object at once. Was it not for the sake of the international and interdenominational bonds of Christian fellowship uniting Swiss and German supporters in World War I that the Basel Mission Society was in World War I finally willing to sacrifice its mission fields in Africa and India, and the properties of the Basel Mission Trading Society?[25] This is true. But in a time of virtually universal conflict, this limited internationalism was tried by fire and failed the test. Ironically, even the well-meant efforts of British Christians to preserve the Basel industries for mission purposes only served to delay the cause of justice. Narrow nationalism triumphed over the Christian world mission in World War I, putting an end to the "Great Century" in missions. As a result of this debacle, the Basel Mission Trading Company lost its close and intimate dedication to the cause of mission.

XVII

Comparisons, Conclusions, and Implications

We can note striking similarities as well as significant differences between the Moravian economic activities and those of Basel. These appear in every one of the following areas.

A. HISTORICAL BACKGROUND

1. The Moravian community in Herrnhut and other European centers attracted a high proportion of aristocracy, as well as many artisans. Both classes were prejudiced against trade. This heightened the opposition to commerce, yet made the breakthrough all the more significant when it came. At Basel, on the other hand, the complexion of the supporting community was far more bourgeois. Then too, Basel entered into overseas missions exactly a century later than the Unitas Fratrum. By this time, under the gathering momentum of a mercantile economy and a developing world trade, attitudes toward commercial activities were somewhat more favorable. When Inspector Otto Schott forced the Basel Mission Society to choose between him and economic activities, the board, though it deeply regretted losing his services, opted firmly to retain economic activities as one expression of its mission.

2. Both the Moravians and Basel provided a matrix for economic activities that was pietistic, ecumenical, and international.

3. Commercial activities began in both groups at a time when mission treasuries were heavily in debt. But men of vision arose who

somehow found the resources to make a beginning both because of and in spite of haunting deficits.

4. Both the Moravians and the men of Basel passed through agonizing periods when they searched their consciences as to the validity of certain types of economic activities and their place in the mission. Neither solved the problem on the basis of unthinking compromise or practical expediency. When crises arose, both groups worked the problem out and validated economic activities in missions on a theological basis and in terms of sound mission methodology.

5. Economic activities first appear in both missions not at times of secular decadence, but when the tides of the pietistic spirit were running high, and the force of the stimulus propelled missions into many kinds of activities in many areas of life.

It is false to assume that Pietism in its earlier phases necessarily represented a flight from the secular. There is, of course, an explanation for the rise of this erroneous assumption. In the twentieth century, Pietism grown old frequently appears in the cloak of modern fundamentalism.

B. CHARACTER AND SCOPE

1. Both Moravians and Basel apparently felt that it was more meaningful to engage in serious industrial and commercial enterprise than to be content with training people for participation in it. This lent to their operations a realism, scope, and effectiveness such as hardly any other groups attained in employing economic activities for missions. Both groups apparently discovered that sounder training could often be given in the setting of serious economic competition than in the artificially sheltered environment of a school.

2. In its early days, the Unitas Fratrum was more international, more ecumenical, and therefore also more supple than the Basel Mission Society in dealing with the tensions and crises affecting economic activities.

3. Both groups came to see economic activities not as an addendum, but as an intrinsic part of missions.

4. European Moravians are exceptional among Protestant churches in providing for economic activities in their constitution and bylaws. They do so on the basis of a well-thought-out theology. American Moravians appear to do little more than imitate the

surrounding culture and the fiscal fundamentalism of most American churches. Many American Moravians seem to be urging the world-wide Unitas Fratrum to lop off its economic involvements. Perhaps it is good that this Americanization of the Moravian Church has not yet been everywhere accepted.

5. Moravians demonstrate an even greater flexibility than Basel. They evidence a readiness to use individual, communal, socialist and capitalist approaches as circumstances seem to indicate. They have been willing to let form follow function.

C. ORGANIZATION

1. In both groups the initial impetus for organizing commercial activities came from experienced Christian businessmen.

2. The experience of both groups would seem to indicate that too close an organizational connection between missions and economic activities is not salutary, but that neither is estrangement. While economic activities require separate organization and special governing boards, they should be carried on in a fraternal spirit of dedication to missions.

3. Both groups recruited investment capital from friends of Christian missions. Both were also ready to take part of the initial investment from mission funds.

4. At times, both the Moravians and Basel were hard put to keep economic activities in an auxiliary role. However, on the whole, the Herrnhuters were more successful than Basel in keeping economic activities a means rather than an end. Perhaps this is one reason why Moravians have been able to maintain an economic ministry to the present day.

5. The Moravians were a church, while Basel was a mission society. The structure of a church was apparently better able to sustain the tension introduced by economic activities. When the interests of mission and business diverged, there was no overarching organizational unit in Basel to coordinate their activities and ease the strain.

D. PRINCIPLES AND AIMS

1. With regard to missionary personnel:

a. Both the Moravians and Basel counted as their most important asset Christian workers who believed passionately in Jesus

Christ and his mission and therefore wanted to devote the full profits of their economic activities to his cause.

b. Both had an honored place for the lay Christian in his capacity as producer of goods, services, and profits. Both minimized clericalism.

c. Basel emphasized the formal training of its missionaries including the briefer training it provided for its industrial and commercial missionaries. The church of the twentieth century talks a good game, but on the whole it has failed signally to train most Christian businessmen going overseas for their personal missionary vocation.

Though the Moravians provided less formal training for their artisan missionaries, life in the spiritual warmth of a Moravian community was itself a good religious and communal preparation for missionary service abroad. The *Zeugengnade,* the charismatic witness, which Moravians were accustomed to exercise at home was the best kind of evangelistic rehearsal for mission overseas. Unlike much of the modern church, the Brethren could export evangelistic witness because they had an abundant supply of it at home.

d. The experience of both groups would seem to show that equal treatment in working conditions, including salary, helps maintain good relations between the various categories of missionaries, including those appointed to economic activities. There may be exceptions to this rule—for example, those business people who carry top managerial responsibility. On the other hand, economic activities may make it possible to level up rather than level down, by providing money to pay more adequate salaries to all hands.

Because of their communal pattern of life, the Moravians more consistently treated their missionaries as equals. Only when Basel expanded the business more rapidly than the supply of mission-minded workers allowed, did it offer higher material inducements to business employees. However, this also created a gulf between them and the regular missionaries and contributed eventually to the virtual secularization of economic activities.

e. Economic activities require, above all things, expert management. When necessary, both Basel and the Brethren went outside their own ranks to recruit qualified personnel. Both cases demonstrate that success in economic activities for mission demands people with the necessary talent, training, and experience. Such work calls for specialists and professionals rather than for clerical amateurs.

When the latter dabble in it, they often bring harm to both the mission and economic activities.[1]

2. Principles and aims with regard to indigenous people:

a. Through economic activities, both the Moravians and Basel sought to undergird the livelihood of indigenous people, including converts to the Christian faith.

b. Both groups placed the well-being of the local people ahead of any kind of rigid ideology or structural fundamentalism in economics.

c. Both showed concern for employee welfare. It is remarkable to find that already in the nineteenth century they provided a wide range of employee benefits, including a credit union, health insurance, and a home ownership program.

d. Economic activities were used by both groups to test the sincerity of catechumens and train the baptized in practical Christian living.

e. Both found that new Christians may require a sheltered community favorable to the development of Christian faith and life. Zeisberger's Indian Village provided such a refuge. So did the Basel industrial communities on the Malabar Coast. Perhaps the lack of such sheltered Christian economic communities for selected new Christians is one reason for the discouraging back door losses in modern mission fields such as Japan.

f. Both the Moravians and Basel found that indigenous people often need to be protected from the unprincipled white trader. The competition of missionary traders helped to combat the evils of economic exploitation and the havoc wrought by the alcohol trade.

3. Principles and aims with regard to the secular realm:

a. Neither the Moravians nor Basel surrendered to the terror of secular involvement which some Christians manifest today. Their high degree of spiritual fervor made them get into the world rather than flee it. They used every available means to witness to Jesus Christ and serve people.

b. While the missionary drive of both groups launched them into the world, this ultimately led to a certain accommodation to the world and to a dilution of group values. Economic activities brought them into contact with the surrounding world, and thus promoted secularization. However, paradoxically, the close community life within those economic enterprises also fostered Christian fellowship and the retention of group values. Over all, the cooperative economic activities of such communities probably helped slow down secularization. At any rate, more conventional Christian communities that simply turn their members over to the surrounding economic culture would be hard put to prove that they have resisted the process of secularization more successfully. The reverse is probably true.

c. Neither the Moravians nor Basel was paralyzed by the fear of imposing a European culture. While Zinzendorf constantly cautioned Brethren missionaries against using the "Herrnhut yardstick," they did not hesitate to share their arts and crafts. In the case of the Basel missionaries, it is clear that their tiles were better, their looms more efficient, than the native Indian counterparts. And the Indian people appreciated these unselfishly shared gifts.

The men of Basel, perhaps somewhat ingenuously, entertained the twin purpose of spreading both the gospel and a "beneficent civilization." They saw no antithesis between adjective and noun when they spoke of teaching people "Christian commerce." They believed that the leaven of the gospel had made important contributions to European culture in general and to economic life in particular. The eagerness with which the Third World today is acquiring the material benefits of Western culture would seem to indicate that the men of Basel were not wholly wrong in regardng "European civilization" and "Christian commerce" as media for Christian service to their fellow men.

d. Both groups found it necessary, in the interest of the workers as well as for the sake of their enterprises, to keep pace with technological developments and adopt mass-production methods. Though they were concerned about some aspects of the factory system, particularly the sociological impact, they came to terms with the inevitable. However, they sought to minimize its accompanying evils and maximize its possibilities for good.

e. Both groups boldly entered the market place and set the tone for commercial operations in their area. Preaching alone would not have succeeded in the face of corrupt and unprincipled commercial practices. The power of a good example and the force of economic competition helped them tip the scales.

E. OUTCOME AND RESULTS

1. Both groups demonstrated that economic activities were no

flash in the pan but could survive and prosper in affiliation with one another for long periods of time.

2. Both found economic activities a useful means of providing for or supplementing mission support. Over the years the harvest was fruitful for the mission as well as for the indigenous people.

3. Economic activities proved to be the base and nucleus of the largest and strongest congregations in both groups.

4. Through their entry into the market place, both Basel and the Brethren were significant factors in guiding social change for the benefit of the local people.

5. "Rice Christianity" does not appear to have been a significant concomitant of economic activities in either group. There was far greater risk of that in conventional mission work, in which the people easily become dependent on the missionary's charity. The latter is likely to involve paternalism. Earning one's own living is still the sure road to self-respect and human dignity.

6. Economic activities, like any other mission activity, were accompanied by annoyances, problems, and crises in the experience of both groups.

7. Both groups regarded economic activities as of equal validity with other mission operations, such as educational and medical missions. Both found commercial and industrial enterprises important channels for exerting Christian influence on people's lives.

F. LESSONS FOR TODAY

1. The Christian world mission must feel as compelled to enter into economic activities as into educational and medical work. It does little good in mission schools to educate the head to dream up more desires, unless the hand (or the head) is able to satisfy those wants. It makes little sense to heal diseases in mission hospitals, if the cured patients soon return with the same illnesses caused by malnutrition. Moreover, if the Christian medical mission has contributed so largely to increasing the number of hungry mouths, it has the moral responsibility to help find ways to feed them.[2]

2. Much can be learned from the long and rich experience of the Moravians and the Basel Mission Society regarding the role of missions in economic activities. In most parts of the world today it would be a mistake to repeat their patterns unimaginatively. Forms must be sought that are in better tune with the present. The structure dare not be colonialistic. It must not be headquartered in

the West, remote from the field of operations in the Third World. Economic activities must be the work of the people themselves. And they themselves must play an important, if not leading, role in all management and decision making. While initial capital can profitably be sought in the West, shareholders and other financial supporters must be sought in the Third World itself. The proportion of indigenous investment and support—through shares, for example— should rise as quickly as possible. Noteworthy examples of such newer enterprises are Namasu Ltd. and Waso Ltd. in New Guinea. These mission-sponsored commercial enterprises boast a large proportion of indigenous shareholders. Their decision-making boards are in New Guinea, not in the West.

3. If even the businessmen of Europe are anxious over the American business invasion, it is not difficult to understand the Third World's fear of economic neo-colonialism. Fears of exploitative neo-colonialism and extractive capitalism may lead to a new revolt on the part of the Third World.[3] Christian business people are needed who will guide the world-wide expansion of American business in such a way that it will benefit primarily the indigenous people.

In addition, there is room for Christian businessmen who will organize economic enterprises for the benefit of indigenous people and of indigenous Christian churches. If individual Christians can devote their "secular" business to Christ, why not a group of Christians together? The Executive Service Corps, which enables American businessmen to advise indigenous enterprises abroad, is setting a commendable example.

4. Non-Western churches will never become truly indigenous until they are economically supported from within their own lands. Only so will they win the respect of their own government and society. Only so will they be in a position to survive if support from abroad should suddenly be cut off by political or military catastrophe in Europe and America. German mission leaders can tell us how disastrous it was for their overseas mission when Hitler's government suddenly cut off support.[4]

5. The pattern of indigenous support for the church need not be everywhere the same. It, too, may be poured into many molds. Many countries in the Third World appear to be heading for a mixed economy rather than an exclusive choice of either private enterprise or collective ownership. Just so, the Christian church in the Third

World may have to adopt mixed forms of stewardship even more than the church in the West.

6. The church's reputation for wealth and corruption abroad is grossly exaggerated. That myth was fostered in large part by lay people, notably princes, who stood to profit from the secularization of the church's possessions. They confiscated the possessions of the church, and especially of the religious orders, without, however, taking over the missionary and social service responsibilities that went with them, as Jaroslav Pelikan has pointed out.[5]

Unlike Pelikan, many historians ever since the Reformation have been too easily taken in by the outcries against the church's alleged wealth and corruption without asking sufficiently pointed questions about the economic and political motives of those who profited most from this propaganda.

The plain truth is that the church nearly everywhere in the world is poor—poor in relation to the tasks expected of it. If offerings were poured out on it as generously as criticism is today, the church would perhaps have the resources with which to carry out the assignments which it is being castigated for not fulfilling. If church investments are confiscated, the charitable causes they support may go begging, thus repeating Reformation history.

7. We must face the fact that the more the average Christian in the West prospers materially, the more self-centered he appears to grow. The spiraling prosperity of the richest middle class of Christians in the entire history of the church seems to be drawing them in the direction of materialism, hedonism, and selfishness. In spite of instant communications that bring the sights and sounds of the world's suffering into our homes, withdrawal and neo-isolationism seem to be increasing. Offerings to missions and benevolences seldom reflect adequately the rise in real income of American church members.[6]

The self-centeredness of the affluent American Protestant congregation is so endemic that former Vice-President Hubert Humphrey told the General Assembly of the National Council of Churches of Christ in the U.S.A. that the Protestant and Orthodox churches of the nation spend only about $500 million a year on helping those outside the churches—"only 41 cents a month for everyone who belongs to a church in America." Of the $75,000,000 income of the Protestant churches in Chicago in a recent year, it is estimated that "less than $6,000,000 was spent outside the local congregations where the money was raised."[7]

Once again we may have to look to a small, dedicated group of people like the Moravians, people who will perform heroically in the world mission out of all proportion to their numbers. These charismatic, Spirit-filled individuals will seek every possible channel through which they can make and support their witness. Some will speak the redemptive Good News of Jesus with their lips. Some will serve their fellow man in educational and medical roles. And some will feel called to serve Christ in the market place individually and together. Perhaps these will find their arena within a specific denomination. Or perhaps an auxiliary group will take shape to serve many different churches and missions interested in employing economic activities for Kingdom goals. Since such a group would not be tied exclusively to any single church or mission, it would perhaps be better fitted for ecumenical service and would be subject to less organizational strain. At any rate, whatever specific structure embodies the idea, I am confident that Christian people will arise to dedicate the best of their talent, experience, and labor to economic activities in the manifold mission of God.

Notes

Chapter I

[1] *Die Religion in Geschichte und Gegenwart,* IV, 1004.

Chapter II

[1] *Ecumenical Missionary Conference* (New York: 1900), I, 97.

[2] *Encyclopedia of Religion and Ethics,* VII, 839. John Mott's figures are about the same: "They [the Moravians] have sent out more than 2,000 of their members as foreign missionaries. At the beginning of 1899 they had 379 missionaries (men and women) or one in sixty-six of the communicant members of their home churches in Europe and America" (*The Evangelization of the World in This Generation* [New York: Student Volunteer Movement, 1900], p. 96). However, in three glowing pages on the Moravians, Mott says not one word about the economic activities that helped make this proportion possible.

[3] H. Motel, "Brüderunität," II, 6, *Die Religion in Geschichte und Gegenwart,* I, 1446.

[4] Hans Wagner, *Abraham Dürninger & Co. 1747-1939,* 2nd ed. (Herrnhut: Abraham Dürninger-Stiftung, 1940), p. 11.

[5] The pietistic overseer himself enthusiastically favored and executed the plan of settling the Moravians on the estate. See Erich Beyreuther, *Zinzendorf und Die Sich Allhier Beisammen Finden* (Marburg an der Lahn: Francke, 1959), p. 113.

[6] Gillian Lindt Gollin, *Moravians in Two Worlds: A Study of Changing Communities,* p. 149. This excellent study in comparative sociology came to my attention in time for the final revision of this manuscript.

[7] Wagner, *op. cit.,* pp. 11-12. See also Erich Beyreuther, *op. cit.,* p. 114.

[8] Zinzendorf ascribes the source of their church order to the Greek

Church: "Schreiben an einen Schwedischen Herrn wegen der Nothwendigkeit der Formen und der eigentlichen Beschaffenheit der Mährischen" (Letter dated 14 Feb. 1738, *Büdingsche Sammlung,* I, 634-35). See also Fritz Blanke, *Zinzendorf und die Einheit der Kinder Gottes* (Basel: Heinrich Majer, 1950)—especially chapter III, which treats Zinzendorf's encounter with the liturgy of the Eastern Church on the basis of his London hymnal and his litanies (pp. 54 ff.). Zinzendorf grew up at Halle under the influence of Francke, who had founded his *Seminarium Orientale* in 1702, and there the love for the Eastern Church had been planted in his soul (*ibid.,* p. 60).

9 RGG, I, 1439 f.

10 Karl Müller, *200 Jahre Brüdermission,* I, *Das erste Jahrhundert* (Herrnhut: Verlag der Missionsbuchhandlung, 1931), 11.

11 Kay Larsen, *Dansk Vestindien* (Copenhagen: C. A. Reitzels Forlag, 1927), p. 78. Cited in Jens Larsen, *Virgin Islands Story* (Philadelphia: Muhlenberg, 1950), p. 63.

12 Müller, *op. cit.,* p. 12.

13 *Ibid.,* p. 7.

14 Otto Uttendörfer, *Alt-Herrnhut: Wirtschaftsgeschichte und Religionssoziologie Herrnhuts während der ersten zwanzig Jahre (1722-42)* (Herrnhut: Missionsbuchhandlung, 1925), p. 14.

15 Count Zinzendorf himself visited St. Thomas in 1739. As his ship entered the harbor, he was worried about the terrible death rate among the first pioneers. Turning to one of his companions, Georg Weber, a Moravian by birth, he asked, "Suppose the brethren are no longer here; what shall we do?" Instantly came the reply: "In that case we are here." The calm steadfastness of Weber, so characteristic of the Moravians' *Zeugengnade,* that witness spirit which Zinzendorf admired all his life, led the Count to exclaim: "An indestructible race, these Moravians!" See J. Taylor Hamilton and Kenneth G. Hamilton, *History of the Moravian Church: The Renewed Unitas Fratrum 1722-1957* (Bethlehem, Pa.: Moravian Church in America, 1967), p. 49.

Chapter III

1 *Alt-Herrnhut: Wirtschaftsgeschichte und Religionssoziologie Herrnhuts während der ersten zwanzig Jahre (1722-42).*

2 John R. Weinlick, *Count Zinzendorf* (Nashville: Abingdon, 1956), p. 212.

3 See Edward Langton, *History of the Moravian Church* (London: Moravian Publication Office, 1895), p. 157 for a demonstration of the Count's personal hesitancy with regard to trade.

4 Hermann Kellenbenz, "German Aristocratic Entrepreneurship: Economic Activities of the Holstein Nobility in the Sixteenth and Seventeenth Centuries," *Explorations in Entrepreneurial History,* VI (1953), 103-14. While this interesting essay describes an important early exception, it does not allow one to generalize that the aristocracy favored trade. As a matter of fact, the author demonstrates that by the seventeenth century Holstein nobles came to feel that trade was unsuitable for their position.

5 Gillian Lindt Gollin, *Moravians in Two Worlds: A Study of Changing Communities,* p. 135. This excellent socio-economic study sheds much light on the motives and dynamics of Moravian society in its economic activities.

6 Martin Luther reflects the general traditional bias of the church against trade and commerce in favor of agriculture and handcraft. The Lutheran background of Zinzendorf influenced him more deeply at that point than the more sympathetic approach of John Calvin toward business. See Andre Bieler, *Gottes Gebot und der Hunger der Welt—Calvin, Prophet des industriellen Zeitalters. Grundlage und Methode der Sozialethik Calvins* (Zurich: EVZ Verlag, 1966), p. 12.

7 "Memorandum of Zinzendorf," September 24, 1749, Moravian Archives in Herrnhut, quoted by Otto Uttendörfer, *Wirtschaftsgeist und Wirtschaftsorganisation Herrnhuts und der Brüdergemeine von 1743 bis zum Ende des Jahrhunderts* (Herrnhut: Verlag der Missionsbuchhandlung, 1926), pp. 359-60. Quoted by Gollin, pp. 137-8.

8 Gollin, *op. cit.,* p. 137.

9 *Ibid.,* p. 138.

10 *Ibid.,* p. 129, quoting the *Jüngerhaus Diarium* of June 13, 1751.

11 *Jüngerhaus Diarium,* August 19, 1754, Moravian Archives in Herrnhut, quoted in Uttendörfer, *op. cit.,* p. 50. See Gollin, p. 165.

12 Zeister Synode, May 24, 1746, Moravian Archives, Herrnhut, quoted in Uttendörfer, p. 36. See Gollin, *op. cit.,* p. 168.

13 See also Uttendörfer, *op. cit.,* p. 39.

14 Hans Wagner, *Abraham Dürninger & Co. 1747-1939,* pp. 12-14. Oaths, public office, military service, and trade were against the somewhat ascetic religion the Brethren had brought with them. The heritage of the Unity of the Brethren reaches back to Peter Chelcicky, a forerunner of the Unity, whose thought bears a remarkable similarity to that of Tolstoy. See Peter Brock, *The Political and Social Doctrines of the Unity of Czech Brethren in the Fifteenth and Sixteenth Centuries,* Slavistic Printings and Reprintings, ed. Cornelis H. Van Schooneveld, Nr. XI ('S-Gravenhage: Mouton & Co., 1957), chapter I. Communism of goods was advocated (p. 80). But this was softened, and soon after 1467 the custom of priests' earning a living by manual work became the only surviving remnant of the Unity's earlier communism. Even after more moderate elements triumphed in the so-called "New Unity" (see chapter VII), traders received only qualified approval and continued to be regarded with suspicion (p. 236).

15 Edmund de Schweinitz, *The Financial History of the American Province of the Unitas Fratrum and Its Sustentation Fund* (Bethlehem: Moravian Publication Office, 1877), p. 17.

16 *Brief Spangenbergs an Zinzendorf,* Amersdam, 7 December 1734. Reproduced in F. Stähelin, *Die Mission der Brüdergemeine in Suriname und Berbice im achtzehnten Jahrhundert* (Herrnhut: Verein für Brüdergeschichte und Paramaribo, C. Kersten & Co., n.d.). 3 vols. in 6 parts. This work is largely a collection of original documents. See I, 1, 18-19: "Agriculture and the

essential crafts are the most natural external labor of Christians, in my
opinion," Spangenberg writes as a youthful theologian. Here he reflects an
attitude going all the way back to Aristotle.

17 See Chapt. 8.

18 See Chapt. 7.

19 See Wagner, *op. cit.;* also Herbert Hammer, *Abraham Dürninger: Ein
Herrnhuter Wirtschaftsmensch des achtzehnten Jahrhunderts.*

20 Wagner, *op. cit.,* p. 29. See also Otto Uttendörfer, *Alt-Herrnhut:
Wirtschaftsgeschichte und Religionssoziologie Herrnhuts während der ersten
zwanzig Jahre (1722-1742).*

21 Wagner, *op. cit.,* p. 80.

22 *Ibid.,* pp. 80-81.

23 Dürninger's linen trade not only gave powerful stimulus to linen
weaving in Saxony, but also was the occasion for the establishment of trade as
a support of missions in Surinam.

24 Wagner, *op. cit., passim.*

25 Otto Uttendörfer, *Wirtschaftsgeist und Wirtschaftsorganisation Herrn-
huts und der Brüdergemeine von 1743 bis zum Ende des Jahrhunderts*
(Herrnhut: Verlag der Missionsbuchhandlung, 1926), p. 143. Quoted by
Gollin, *op. cit.,* p. 175.

26 Status der Firma Abraham Dürninger und Co., December 31, 1773,
Dürninger Archiv, Herrnhut, quoted in Uttendörfer, *Wirtschaftsgeist,* p. 143.
Reproduced by Gollin, p. 175.

27 *Ibid.*

28 Bilanzen, Dürninger Archiv, Vol. 12, Herrnhut, quoted in Wagner, *Die
Handlung Dürninger,* pp. 106, 175-76. See also Gollin, p. 176.

29 At the end of World War II the large textile mills, tobacco factories, and
other enterprises found themselves in the Soviet Zone of Germany. Under the
Communist regime, the Abraham Dürninger Foundation has, of course, been
stripped of many of its great enterprises, but still manages to do business,
though on a greatly reduced scale. Meanwhile at Bad Boll, Württemberg, in
West Germany, Dürninger Zigarren GmbH, which operates a chain of sixteen
tobacco stores, has its offices in the same Moravian headquarters building in
which the mission executive suite is found. Other Moravian interests in West
Germany include a resort hotel at Bad Boll for church conferences and a
department store.

30 Gollin, *op. cit.,* p. 196.

31 *Ibid.,* p. 171.

32 *Ibid.,* p. 172.

33 *Ibid.,* p. 177.

34 Fulneck, between Leeds and Bradford, was a chief settlement, including
schools, choir houses, and industries. See Erich Beyreuther, *Nikolaus Ludwig
von Zinzendorf* (Reinbeck bei Hamburg: Rowohlt, 1965), p. 129.

35 Edward Langton, *History of the Moravian Church,* p. 145.

36 "To the Moravian Church, More Especially that Part of it now or lately residing in England," June 24, 1744, *Büdingsche Sammlung,* III, 1021-22. The full text is available in *The Letters of the Reverend John Wesley, A.M.,* Ed. John Telford (London: Epworth Press, 1931), II, 22.

Chapter IV

1 Edmund de Schweinitz, S.T.D., *The Financial History of the American Province of the Unitas Fratrum and Its Sustentation Fund* (Bethlehem: Moravian Publication Office, 1877), p. 15.

2 The best and most complete general history is the increasingly rare three-volume work by Joseph Mortimer Levering, *The History of Bethlehem 1741-1892* (Bethlehem, Pennsylvania: Times Publishing Co., 1903). Levering, a bishop of the Moravian Church, wrote this history for the sesquicentennial of the Moravian Congregation at Bethlehem.

3 See De Schweinitz, *op. cit.*

4 Jacob John Sessler, *Communal Pietism among Early American Moravians* (New York: Henry Holt, 1933), p. 92.

5 Bishop August Gottlieb Spangenberg ordered that artisans should charge the market price. Helmuth Erbe, *Bethlehem, Pennsylvania: Eine Kommunistische Herrnhuter Kolonie des 18. Jahrhunderts,* p. 165. This is in marked contrast to the Rule of Benedict which had prescribed that monastery artisans of the Benedictine order should avoid all appearance of greed by charging somewhat less than the regular market price. This well-meant price-cutting invited the hostility of the craft guilds with the rise of towns in Europe.

6 See also Gollin, *Moravians in Two Worlds,* p. 156.

7 Erbe, *op. cit.,* p. 165.

8 Gollin, *op. cit.,* p. 156.

9 *Ibid.,* p. 158.

10 *Ibid.,* p. 161.

11 *Ibid.,* p. 178.

12 *Zinzendorf und die Christenheit* (Marburg an der Lahn: Francke, 1961), p. 225.

13 Otto Uttendörfer, *Zinzendorfs religiöse Grundgedanken* (Herrnhut: Verlag der Missionsbuchhandlung, 1935), p. 152.

14 Gollin, *op. cit.,* p. 18.

15 Early Bethlehem is very well described by Helmuth Erbe, *op. cit.*

16 *Das Evangelium auf dem Wege zum Menschen* (Berlin: Evangelische Verlagsanstalt, 1961), p. 234.

17 *Instruction an alle Heyden-Boten. 1738. Büdingsche Sammlung,* II, 672.

18 Two apprentices who had "no heart for the Savior and the community" and therefore did not want to stay were permitted to leave. The leaders of the community did not want to go to law, and instead tore up the indenture papers and let them go (*Conferenz Protocoll der Committee in Bethlehem von*

1762 bis d. 3ten May 1780, Archives of the Moravian Church, Bethlehem, Pennsylvania).

19 Even after the strictly communist phase was over and Bethlehem had passed into a more socialist pattern, the *consileum abeundi* was given rather frequently, as is evident from the *Conferenz Protocoll.* In most cases dismissal was effective immediately and the expellees had to leave Bethlehem on the same day. In the case of a certain Peter Volz, who was expelled because of "intolerably bad conduct," his master, Brother Huber, undertook to see to it that he was apprenticed to another good master with whom he could learn the blacksmith trade (*Conferenz Protocoll,* 28 January 1768, p. 112).

The community could be selective about whom it would accept. The leaders turned down a mentally retarded man who insisted on joining the community. Because he would not go willingly, someone had to go with him to New York and put him on a ship (*Conferenz Protocoll,* 18 February 1763, pp. 42-43).

20 Sessler, *op. cit.,* p. 87.

21 Elma E. Gray, *Wilderness Christians: The Moravian Missions to the Delaware Indians,* p. 21.

22 Sessler, *op. cit.,* p. 188.

23 Gollin, *op. cit.,* p. 159.

24 *Ibid.,* p. 200.

25 *Ibid.,* pp. 200-01.

26 *Ibid.,* p. 97.

27 *Ibid.,* p. 209.

28 Sessler, *op. cit.,* p. 209.

29 Gollin, *op. cit.,* pp. 221-22, 225.

30 *Ibid.,* p. 18.

31 Max Weber, *The Protestant Ethic and the Spirit of Capitalism,* tr. T. Parsons (London: George Allen & Unwin Ltd., 1930), p. 175. Gollin, however, (p. 197) fails to include the remedy which Wesley added to this otherwise gloomy outlook: "What way, then, can we take, that our money may not sink us to the nethermost hell? There is one way, and there is no other under heaven. If those who *gain* all they can, and *save* all they can, will likewise *give* all they can, then the more they gain the more they will grow in grace, and the more treasure they will lay up in heaven." Robert Southey, *Life of Wesley and the Rise and Progress of Methodism,* 2 vols. (New York: Evert Duyckinck and George Long, 1820), II, 236. Wesley himself obeyed this maxim throughout his long life, giving an estimated £30,000 to charity. This is an outstanding example of economic activity devoted to charity, for Wesley earned the money largely by serving as his own printer and bookseller.

Chapter V

1 Karl Müller, *200 Jahre Brüdermission,* I, *Das erste Jahrhundert,* 26.

2 J. E. Hutton, *A Short History of the Moravian Church* (London: Moravian Publication Office, 1895), p. 152.

3 Müller, *op. cit.,* p. 28.

4 *Ibid.*

5 *Ibid.,* p. 27.

6 Gollin, *Moravians in Two Worlds,* p. 154.

7 Enrico C. S. Molnar, "The Pious Fraud of Count Zinzendorf," *The Iliff Review,* XI (Spring, 1954), 35.

8 John R. Weinlick, *Count Zinzendorf,* p. 100.

9 Zinzendorf, *Zurückgelassenes Eventual-Testament an die Gemeine, bey des Herrn Gr. v.Z. ersten Reise nach America, Anno 1738. Büdingsche Sammlung,* II, 266, tr. mine.

10 *Ibid.,* pp. 266-67.

11 Wagner, *Abraham Dürninger & Co.,* p. 21.

12 *Büdingsche Sammlung,* II, 267.

13 De Schweinitz, *The Financial History of the American Province of the Unitas Fratrum and Its Sustentation Fund* (Bethlehem: Moravian Publication Office, 1877), p. 5.

14 August Gottlieb Spangenberg, *Von der Arbeit der evangelischen Brüder unter den Heiden* (Barby: Christian Friedrich Laux, 1782), pp. 84-85. This is a veritable manual of Moravian missionary methods tested by almost fifty years of pioneer experience. The common household had deep religious roots among the Brethren, but it also demonstrated its worth in helping the Moravians survive and work effectively in inhospitable primitive surroundings. Interestingly, this is the type of economy favored by many primitive societies in similar settings.

15 Augustus C. Thompson, *Moravian Missions,* p. 476.

16 E. Lord, *A Compendious History of the Principal Protestant Missions to the Heathen,* I, 235.

17 Thompson, *op. cit.,* p. 475.

18 This concept attached first to the martyr and then to the ascetic. There was more than a trace of asceticism in the roots of the Brethren in the fifteenth century. This was one factor among others which prepared the soil for the seed of the "Streiteridee," the *militia Christi* concept which Zinzendorf articulated and which was expressed by the so-called "Losungen," or password for the day, a practice first begun in 1728 and continuing today (Erich Beyreuther, *Nikolaus Ludwig von Zinzendorf,* p. 75).

Today, the *Losungen* are circulated far beyond the small European Moravian membership of 10,000 to 11,000 members. In the two political divisions of Germany about one million copies are circulated, and in other parts of Europe an additional 200,000. Zinzendorf followed no model in his work. He was a brilliant improviser according to the needs of a given situation and the available resources, as Beyreuther has shown, EMZ, 17 (1960), pp. 102 ff. However, his whole accent on working and fighting for Christ has many similarities to the missionary monasticism of the Middle Ages.

19 Zinzendorf, *Eventual-Testament, Büdingsche Sammlung,* II, 279, tr. mine.

20 Herman Carl Lawaetz, *Brodremenighedens Missionshistorie* (Copenhagen: Wroblevski, 1902), p. 144.

21 *Ibid.,* pp. 257-58.

22 Here they were in the tradition of the early church, which runs along similar lines, as demonstrated by Hans von Campenhausen in his essay, "Die Christen und das bürgerliche Leben," *Tradition und Leben, Kräfte der Kirchengeschichte* (Tübingen: Mohr, 1960), pp. 180-202. See esp. the conclusion on p. 202.

23 *Instruction der Brüder, die unter die Russischen Heiden (Samojeten) gegangen.* 1736. A complete text with apparatus for textual criticism of the various versions is reproduced in O. Uttendörfer, *Die wichtigsten Missionsinstruktionen Zinzendorfs. Hefte zur Missionskunde Nr. 12,* pp. 9-13. The slavemasters, of course, did not want their slaves to be educated.

24 August Gottlieb Spangenberg, *Von der Arbeit der evangelischen Brüder unter den Heiden* (Barby: Christian Friedrich Laux, 1782), p. 62.

25 *Ibid.,* pp. 62-63.

26 *Leben des Herrn Nicolaus Ludovig Grafen und Herrn von Zinzendorf und Pottendorf.* 3 vols., XII, 1271. Volumes I and II carry no date of publication, volume III is dated 1774. In lieu of a publisher's name, all three are simply imprinted, "Zu finden in den Brüdergemeinen."

27 Erich Beyreuther, *Zinzendorf und die Christenheit 1732-1760* (Marburg an der Lahn: Francke, 1961), p. 175.

28 J. Taylor Hamilton and Kenneth G. Hamilton, *History of the Moravian Church,* p. 258.

29 J. V. Daele, "Letter to 'Syn Exfelentie Graaf v. Sinsendorpp,' " dated 12 September 1742, at St. Thomas, *Büdingsche Sammlung,* III, 480-81. There were also other occasions on which the Brethren purchased the freedom of slaves.

30 Thompson, *op. cit.,* pp. 484-85.

31 *Ibid.,* p. 484.

Chapter VI

1 Spangenberg, *Von der Arbeit der evangelischen Brüder unter den Heiden,* pp. 138-39.

2 This practice began very early in the Moravian work among the Indians. Already in 1743 a Moravian diary records that on April 19 the missionaries were giving the Indians suggestions for their spring planting ("Diarium der Heyden-Boten unter den Indianern in Shecomeko, 8/19 August, 1743," *Büdingsche Sammlung,* II, 255). But the missionaries taught by example as well, working in their own fields for their own support (*ibid.,* p. 257).

3 R. Pierce Beaver, *Church, State, and the American Indians* (St. Louis: Concordia Publishing House, 1966), p. 20. This excellent study deserves to be far better known than it is at present.

[4] While intoxicated, the Indians of Shekomeko, New York, had sold their lands for a trifle. After their conversion the converts were driven from their lands. The Brethren helped them by buying land for them on the Mahoning River in Pennsylvania. The same happened with regard to the Indians at Wechquadnach and Meniolagomekah (Spangenberg, *op. cit.*, pp. 141-42).

[5] *Statutes agreed upon by the Christian Indians, at Languntouteniink and Welhik-Tuppeek, in the month of August, 1772.* Original ms. Bethlehem Archives. Quoted in full by Edmund de Schweinitz, *The Life and Times of David Zeisberger,* pp. 378-79.

[6] *Ibid.,* pp. 316-318.

[7] *Protokoll der Missions-Conferenz, gehalten in Gosen am Muskingum, vom 10ten bis zum 21ten Oct. 1803.* Original minutes in German by Benjamin Mortimer, Archives of the Moravian Church, Bethlehem, Pennsylvania, Box 174, Folio 1.

[8] *Diary of Goschgoschünk and Lawunakhanek, February 25-September 7, 1769.* Original by David Zeisberger, Archives of the Moravian Church, Bethlehem, Pennsylvania. See entries for May 12, 1769. No wonder Zeisberger early appreciated the benefits of a Christian Town, as he declares in the diary under date of May 24, 1769.

[9] *Diary of the Indian congregation at Goshen on the river Muskingum from 1st May to 31st October, 1800,* Archives of the Moravian Church, Bethlehem, Pennsylvania. See entries under May 1, 1800, p. 1.

[10] *Ibid.,* May 4, 1800, p. 2.

[11] *Diary of the Indian Congregation at Goshen on the Muskingum, from June 1, 1801, to May 31, 1802.* Original English by Benjamin Mortimer, entry under April 24, 1802, p. 52, Archives of the Moravian Church, Bethlehem, Pennsylvania.

[12] See Beaver, chapter 2, "Indian Missions in the New Nation," for a good historical summary. It was not until 1819 that Congress established a permanent "Civilization Fund" with an appropriation of $10,000. The act authorized the President "to employ capable persons of good moral character, to instruct the Indians in the mode of agriculture suitable to their situation; and for teaching their children in reading, writing, and arithmetic. . . ." To help the money go as far as possible, the act courted the help of Christian missionaries. But this development was much too late to help David Zeisberger and the harried remnant that clung to him. However, the government's eventual partnership with missions in a program of civilization was an ipso facto endorsement of Eliot, the Mayhews, Zeisberger, and other missionaries.

[13] *Diary of the Indian Congregation at Goshen on the Muskingum, from June 1, 1801, to May 31, 1802.* Original English ms. by Benjamin Mortimer, Archives of the Moravian Church, Bethlehem, Pennsylvania. See entry for May 8, 1802, p. 53. The initial ambiguous stance of the American government contrasts with the solid support which Roman Catholic missionaries received from the Spanish crown in their mission to the Indians.

[14] The first massacre of Moravian Indians, attended by the murder of a number of Moravian missionaries, took place at the hands of Indians in the

service of the French during the French and Indian Wars, when Gnadenhütten on the Mahoning was attacked November 24, 1755. This tragedy helped dispel the suspicions English settlers were directing at the Christian Indian town near Bethlehem (Karl Müller, *200 Jahre Brüdermission*, I, *Das erste Jahrhundert* [Herrnhut: Missionsbuchhandlung, 1931], pp. 223 ff.).

15 A good diagram of the wanderings of the "pilgrim church" is found in Müller, *op. cit.*, p. 245.

16 The best and most available account of the wanderings of the "pilgrim church," as well as of the massacre, is Elma E. Gray's *Wilderness Christians: The Moravian Mission to the Delaware Indians* (Ithaca, New York: Cornell University Press, 1956).

17 An extended account is found in the even-handed treatment of Edmund de Schweinitz, pp. 537-557. While criticizing the settlers, he is also very fair in describing the Indian and British forays which contributed to their inflamed state of mind.

18 Gray, *op. cit.*, p. 74.

19 Beaver, *op. cit.*, p. 58.

20 The Indians themselves, in common with other primitive societies in many parts of the world, kept prisoners of war as slaves. These included members of other tribes as well as whites.

Chapter VII

1 Paul A. Theile, communication of October 2, 1967 to the author.

2 Müller, *200 Jahre Brüdermission*, I, pp. 145-49. Zinzendorf apparently had been skeptical of the venture from the beginning. Ever since the catastrophic experience of St. Croix, he was opposed to any combination of colonization with mission or anything that resembled it (*ibid.*, p. 147).

3 F. W. Peacock, "The Moravian Mission in Labrador," *Canadian Geographic Journal*, LX (May, 1960), 185. Copies of the Royal Proclamations are deposited in the Public Archives in St. John's, Newfoundland.

4 H. Anthony Williamson, "The Moravian Mission and Its Impact on the Labrador Eskimo," *Arctic Anthropology*, II (Madison, Wisconsin: 1964), pp. 32-33.

5 *Ibid.*, p. 32.

6 *Ibid.*, p. 33.

7 Alfred Gysin, *Mission im Heimatland der Eskimos* (Hamburg: Ludwig Appel, 1966), p. 8. This is a good, brief, up-to-date account of the Moravian mission to Labrador, thus supplementing *200 Jahre Brüdermission.*

8 See Spangenberg, *Von der Arbeit der evangelischen Brüder,* p. 115.

9 Müller, *op. cit.*, p. 158.

10 Spangenberg, *op. cit.*, p. 82.

11 Müller, *op. cit.*, p. 315.

12 See Spangenberg, pp. 150-168, for a report on the renewal of the society and a complete text of its constitution as of 1768.

13 *Ibid.,* p. 163.

14 *Ibid.,* p. 164, tr. mine.

15 *Ibid.,* pp. 157ff.

16 *Ibid.,* p. 159.

17 A detailed account of the continuing relation between mission and trade in the Moravian mission to Labrador is found in Adolf Schulze's *200 Jahre Brüdermission,* II, *Das Zweite Jahrhundert,* 50-55.

18 Gysin, *op. cit.,* p. 15.

19 *Ibid.,* p. 20.

20 From 1870 the Moravian trade with Labrador required two ships simultaneously. One of these supplementary trading vessels was lost in 1881 at the mouth of the Thames. Apparently this was the only disaster in the entire period from 1770 to 1926. See Gysin, *op. cit.,* p. 32.

21 Adolph Schulze and S. H. Gapp, *World-Wide Moravian Missions* (Bethlehem, Pennsylvania: Comenius Press, 1926), pp. 22-25. A much earlier Protestant effort at trading for mission support in Massachusetts did not work out well. Goods were sent to Boston for sale by the Society for the Propagation of the Gospel in New England (New England Company). See William Kellaway, *The New England Company, 1649-1776* (New York: Barnes and Noble, 1962).

22 Gysin, *op. cit.,* p. 32.

23 Hamilton and Hamilton, *History of the Moravian Church,* p. 268.

24 *Ibid.,* p. 501.

25 Schulze, *op. cit.,* p. 53.

26 Hamilton and Hamilton, *op. cit.,* p. 503.

27 Gysin, *op. cit.,* p. 40.

28 Gysin declares: "The confidence of the Eskimo in their missionaries rose again after the latter no longer had anything to do with trade" (p. 43).

29 Hamilton and Hamilton, *op. cit.,* p. 508.

30 Schulze, *op. cit.,* p. 55.

31 Gysin, *op. cit.,* p. 47.

32 Gysin, "Die Probleme für die Zukunft Labradors," *op. cit.,* pp. 60-64.

Chapter VIII

1 F. Stähelin, *Die Mission der Brüdergemeine in Suriname und Berbice im achtzehnten Jahrhundert,* I, pp. 7-9.

2 Albert Helman, *Merchant, Mission and Meditation: The Romance of a Two Hundred Year Old Suriname Company,* pp. 60, 82, 84. This is a candid and thoughtful volume, far above the usual level of house histories. Albert Helman is the pen name of a famous Dutch author, born and raised in Surinam. In real life he is referred to as His Excellency Doctor Lou Lichtveld, Netherlands envoy extraordinary and minister plenipotentiary, delegate to the

General Assembly of the United States. This imperfect, at times awkward translation of the Dutch edition does not do full justice to the original.

3 *The Advance Guard: 200 Years of Moravian Missions 1732-1932* (London: Moravian Book Room, 1932), pp. 38-39. The author, who is identified only with the initials "A.W.," says that he has adapted his materials from Bishop S. Baudert's *Auf der Hut des Herrn* (Herrnhut, 1931).

4 Schulze and Gapp, *World-Wide Moravian Missions,* p. 159.

5 Beginning with 1756 the *Heidendiakonie* struggled with virtually annual deficits rising to 9000 Taler by 1760 (Müller, *200 Jahre Brüdermission,* I, pp. 318-19).

6 Excerpt from the minutes of the mission board (Johs. v. Watteville, Kornelis van Laar, Nathan Seidel and J. P. Weiss), April 23, 1758, at Herrnhut (Stähelin, II, pt. 3, 130-131).

7 Herbert Hammer, *Abraham Dürninger: Ein Herrnhuter Wirtschaftsmensch des achtzehnten Jahrhunderts,* p. 34.

8 Zander to Saalwaechter, Paramaribo, 24 January (1757?) (Stähelin, II, pt. 3, 80).

9 Jonas Paul Weiss, "Letter to the Brethren and Sisters in Surinam," dated April 1758 at Herrnhut (*ibid.,* p. 134).

10 *Ibid.*

11 In spite of the example of Dürninger's successful linen export business in Herrnhut, it was some time before Weiss's ideas carried the day. In 1765 the same mission board which had sent out the chest of striped linen for sale in 1758, resolved to make a new start in Paramaribo (the Brethren had either died or returned home in the meantime), but this new Brethren settlement in accordance with a resolution of the synod was allowed only to conduct handcrafts, no commercial business. However, Christoph Kersten, a tailor who arrived in 1765, gave his name to the business in 1768, and as time went on it branched out into many types of the originally forbidden "commercial business." See C. Kersten & Co., *In Commemoration 1768-1918* (Paramaribo, 1918).

12 Helman, *op. cit.,* p. 75.

13 Schulze, *200 Jahre Brüdermission,* II, p. 338.

14 Helman, *op. cit.,* p. 100.

15 *Ibid.,* p. 101.

16 *Ibid.,* p. 98.

17 *Ibid.,* p. 97.

18 *Ibid.,* pp. 110-112.

19 *Ibid.,* p. 114.

20 *Ibid.,* p. 70.

21 *Ibid.,* p. 106.

22 *Ibid.,* p. 118.

23 *Ibid.,* p. 119.

24 *Ibid.,* p. 123.

25 Compiled on the basis of figures in Schulze, *200 Jahre Brüdermission,* II, p. 339.

26 *Ibid.*

27 One is reminded of a large farm in Tanganyika which was the economic salvation of a German Lutheran mission cut off from all support by Hitler.

28 Helman, *op. cit.,* p. 151.

29 *Ibid.,* p. 141.

30 *Ibid.,* p. 140.

31 *Ibid.,* p. 138.

32 *Ibid.,* p. 139.

33 *Ibid.,* p. 196.

34 *Ibid.,* pp. 192-206.

35 J. de Kraker in a letter to the author dated May 26, 1964, at Paramaribo. De Kraker, a non-Moravian, is manager of C. Kersten and Co.

36 Schulze, *200 Jahre,* p. 337.

37 The beginnings of this social welfare work are described by Siegfried Beck, *Die Wirtschaftlich-soziale Arbeit der Missionsgeschäfte der Brüdergemeine in Suriname,* Hefte zur Missionskunde Nr. 14 (Herrnhut: Missionsbuchhandlung, 1914). The management of C. Kersten & Co. requested the permission of the mission director to use a part of their profits to initiate social welfare work.

38 Schulze, *200 Jahre,* pp. 338-39.

39 Helman, *op. cit.,* p. 61.

40 *Ibid.,* p. 70.

41 Hamilton and Hamilton, *History of the Moravian Church,* p. 564.

42 Helman, *op. cit.,* pp. 164ff.

43 *Ibid.,* p. 147.

44 *Ibid.,* p. 136.

45 *Ibid.,* p. 183.

46 *Church Order of the Unitas Fratrum (Moravian Church) 1957. Published by Order of the General Synod Held at Bethlehem, Pennsylvania. August 13-September 10, 1957* (Bethlehem, Pennsylvania, 1958).

47 Helman, *op. cit.,* p. 154.

48 *Ibid.,* p. 133.

49 *Ibid.,* pp. 190, 213.

50 *Ibid.,* p. 103.

51 *Ibid.,* p. 170.

52 *Ibid.,* p. 145.

53 *Ibid.,* p. 153.

54 *Ibid.,* p. 145.

55 *Ibid.,* p. 209.

56 *Ibid.,* p. 215.

57 *Ibid.,* pp. 210, 216.

58 *Ibid.,* p. 214.

Chapter IX

1 Zinzendorf had mixed feelings about Georg Schmidt, who had been imprisoned for his evangelical faith but apparently had been released only on his declaration that he was a Roman Catholic. Schmidt was already on his way to South Africa, but since he was delayed in Holland, Zinzendorf sent him a letter with additional instructions. He writes with utmost frankness: "If you were not an exceptional person, I would lose my mind over you. Your denial of your Savior and His cause would worry me that you would perish. But now I hope. The one thing that disturbs me is your attitude. You cannot possibly adduce Peter's [denial] to your advantage, for Peter nearly cried his eyes out, but you thought you did right. I do not doubt that you have since then suffered a thousand times more anxiety than Peter, but the question is, whether the eyes of Jesus were the motive or the attitude of the Brethren?" ("Kurze Instruction vor meinem Br. Schmidt nach Cabo, 1736," Uttendörfer, *Die Wichtigsten Missionsinstruktionen Zinzendorfs,* pp. 13-14, tr. mine). A similar reference to Schmidt is found in a statement Zinzendorf made at the Synod at Gotha in 1740: "Brother Schmidt at the Cape was of no use in the congregation [at Herrnhut] and in a few weeks he had 20, 30 Hottentots, who were at least listening to him. . ." (*ibid.,* p. 32). On the one hand we see here that missions could sometimes be a way of exporting problem cases from Herrnhut. On the other hand, Zinzendorf gives further expression to his rising esteem for Schmidt in his one-sentence ordination by letter to the ministry: "In view of the possibility of a baptism or a communion I ordain you, who are an apostle of the Lamb far superior to myself, as a servant of our Church in the Name of the Father, the Son and the Holy Spirit. Amen" ("Ordinationsbrief Zinzendorfs und G. Schmidt, 1741," *ibid.,* p. 16, tr. mine).

2 This was a marked departure from the usual Moravian practice.

3 Schulze and Gapp, *World-wide Moravian Missions,* pp. 91-95, *passim.* The writer was privileged to visit Genadendal in 1970.

4 *Ibid.,* p. 97.

5 Augustus C. Thompson, *Moravian Missions* (New York: Charles Scribner's Sons, 1882), p. 396.

6 *Ibid.,* p. 404.

7 Secretary of Moravian Missions, Basel, Switzerland (Paul A. Theile in a letter to the author dated March 3, 1964).

8 *Ibid.*

9 *Ibid.*

10 *Ibid.*

11 Schulze and Gapp, *op. cit.,* p. 97.

[12] E. van Calker, *Die Grant-Stationen in Süd-Afrika.* Hefte zur Missions-Kunde Nr. 5 (Herrnhut: Missionsbuchhandlung, 1909), p. 4.

[13] *Ibid.,* pp. 2-3.

[14] *Ibid.,* p. 4.

[15] *Ibid.,* p. 1. The Rhenish properties were twelve times as large as those of the Moravians.

[16] The situation became even more intolerable after the missionary first lost his police powers; for a time he continued to have the responsibility for law and order without the authority to enforce it (*ibid., p. 12*).

[17] *Ibid.,* p. 9.

[18] *Ibid.,* p. 8. From concrete instances such as this, one gains a new appreciation of the basic wisdom of Luther's distinction between the "drei Stände." In South Africa the missionaries, through force of circumstance rather than by choice, had to perform the functions of all three orders, including care for the people's physical and economic welfare. This has frequently been the case where missionaries have been the only representatives of advanced culture in contact with primitive people. And Martin Luther would be the first to say that by being primarily in one "Stand," e.g., the clergy, one does not cease being a member of the other two; for the human being is, in the final analysis, indivisible.

[19] Schulze, *200 Jahre Brüdermission,* II, p. 436.

[20] Van Calker, *op. cit.,* pp. 15 f. Van Calker was president of the Moravian mission in Eastern South Africa and played an important part in the negotiations with the government which he describes. This makes him an especially valuable source.

[21] Schulze, *200 Jahre,* II, pp. 436-37.

Chapter X

[1] F. P. Stocker, President of the Provincial Elders' Conference (Executive Board) of the Moravian Church in America, Northern Province, Letter to the author dated January 8, 1964.

[2] *Die Grundsätze der Evangelischen Brüder-Unität (Herrnhuter Brüdergemeine) verbindlich fur die beiden Verwaltungsbereiche Deutsche Brüder-Unität mit dem Sitz in Herrnhut/Oberlausitz (Distrikt Herrnhut) und Europäische Festländische Brüder-Unität mit dem Sitz in Bad Boll/ Württemberg (Distrikt Bad Boll) vom Jahre 1959* (Herrnhut, 1961), p. 28.

[3] *Ibid.,* "2 Abschnitt. Die Einzelgemeinde innerhalb der Europäisch-Festländischen Brüder-Unität, III, Das Zeugnis des Lebens," p. 29.

[4] *Ibid.,* p. 46.

[5] *The Encyclopedia of Religion and Ethics,* VIII, 838.

[6] One of these auxiliaries was the Society for the Furtherance of the Gospel, organized in 1741 to serve Moravian missionaries en route to and from the field. It ultimately became the mission arm of the British Moravian Church, and is still at work today. Others include the Zeist Mission Society in

the Netherlands (1793), the Wachovian Brethren Society in Salem, North
Carolina (1823), and numerous smaller groups in Europe and America. The
largest auxiliary among non-Moravians is the London Association in Aid of the
Mission of the United Brethren (1817) (Schulze, *200 Jahre,* II, pp. 669-71).

The Society for the Propagation of the Gospel, founded at Bethlehem
(1787), still serves as an investment agency and holding corporation for the
American Province, North, and gives its proceeds to the Board of Foreign
Missions of the Moravian Church in America, Inc. The Foreign Missionary
Society of the Moravian Church, South, serves the same function in the
Southern American Province (The Board of Foreign Missions of the Moravian
Church in America, Inc., *The Gospel under Palm and Pine; 1965 Annual
Report* [Bethlehem, Pa.: The Board of Foreign Missions of the Moravian
Church in America, Inc., 1966]).

7 Zinzendorf, *Instruction an alle Heyden-Boten,* 1738. Found in *Büdingsche Sammlung,* II, 672-73. In Labrador this system continued as late as 1907.
The Moravian example impressed other noted Protestant pioneers, especially
William Carey. He advocated the Moravian model of self-support and common
household in his famous *Enquiry into the Obligations of Christians to Use
Means for the Conversion of the Heathens.* In India he vigorously carried out
the Moravian plan with one significant adaptation: While the Moravians
appointed a permanent house father for each common household, Carey's
Serampore Trio each served as house father a month at a time on a rotating
basis.

8 Müller, *200 Jahre Brüdermission,* I, p. 219.

9 Schulze, *200 Jahre Brüdermission,* II, pp. 86-87, describes the reintro-
duction of reindeer into Alaska by Sheldon Jackson. Jackson, formerly a
Presbyterian missionary to the Indians and secretary of missions, was General
Agent of Education for the U.S. government in Alaska. "Missionaries being the
most intelligent and disinterested friends of the natives," Sheldon regarded
them as "best fitted to wisely plan and carry out methods of transferring the
ownership of the deer from the Government to the natives. . . ." Beginning in
1894, Jackson introduced domestic reindeer from Siberia and Lapland. His
early plans included turning herds over to the Episcopal, Presbyterian, Roman
Catholic, Moravian, Methodist, and Swedish mission stations (Sheldon
Jackson, *Report on Introduction of Domestic Reindeer into Alaska 1894.*
53rd Congress, 3rd Session, Senate, Ex. Doc. No. 92 [Washington: Government Printing Office, 1895], p. 14). In recognition of their efforts at placing
domestic reindeer into the hands of the Eskimos, the mission stations were
given a herd, too. By 1908 the Moravian herd at Bethel numbered 692 head.
By 1914 the reindeer in Alaska numbered 47,266 of which already 30,532 had
passed into Eskimo ownership (Schulze, p. 87). It was Jackson who had
turned to the Moravians in 1883, pleading with them to begin mission work in
Alaska, because he had found no Protestant denomination willing to help the
Eskimos (*ibid.,* p. 90).

10 Müller, *op. cit.,* p. 325. Bishop David Nitschmann, himself a carpenter,
wrote from Pennsylvania in 1741 that masons, smiths, and weavers charged
high prices in America, and that iron articles were twice as expensive as in
Germany (Gray, *Wilderness Christians,* p. 25). As late as 1798 there was not a

single saddler in all of Upper Canada (Goshen, Muskingum, Ohio, Diaries, May 19, 1798).

11 Erbe, *Bethlehem, Pennsylvania,* chapter IIIb.

12 Müller, *op. cit.,* p. 327.

13 For eighteenth-century German pietism, trade in a special sense still represented "the world" from which one should flee (*ibid.,* p. 330). The neo-pietism of the nineteenth century had greater sympathy for trade, as is evidenced by the numerous pietistic merchants and associations of merchants.

14 *Ibid.*

15 C. Buchner, *Acht Monate in Südafrika: Schilderung der dortigen Mission der Brüdergemeine* (Gütersloh: C. Bertelsmann, 1894), pp. 156ff.

16 Müller, *op. cit.,* p. 141.

Chapter XI

1 Wilhelm Schlatter, *Geschichte der Basler Mission,* I, 17.

2 Gustav Adolf Wanner, *Die Basler Handelsgesellschaft,* pp. 19-20.

3 *Die Religion in Geschichte und Gegenwart,* I, 1729-30.

4 It was formed at the suggestion of Christian Friedrich Spittler (1792-1867), who had been secretary of the *Deutsche Christentumsgesellschaft* in Basel since 1801. The Basel Mission Society was only one of many projects his fertile imagination conceived (RGG, VI, 260).

5 On the other hand, one could perhaps argue that the Unitas Fratrum was likewise a total church become a pietistic club. While the Moravians welded Christians of diverse backgrounds together in a witnessing church subscribing to the Augsburg Confession, Zinzendorf in his concept of various "tropes" of the Unitas Fratrum also provided for a Reformed trope. The Continental groups accept both the Augsburg Confession and the Heidelberg Catechism, the English-speaking groups both the Augsburg Confession and the Thirty-nine Articles.

6 I recognize that the distinction between Basel as a mission society and the Moravians as a church is less than perfect, since a wide circle of sympathetic Christians in the large territorial churches used the Moravian Church as their channel of support for missions in much the same way as many Christians in the large churches used the mission societies.

7 Since the Basel Mission Society was from the first oriented toward training missionaries for the English and Dutch societies, it is probable that Basel was also greatly influenced by the example of the London Missionary Society and its artisan missionaries. Urlsperger had visited England shortly before he founded the *Deutsche Christentumsgesellschaft,* which maintained ties with the London Missionary Society.

8 Schlatter, *op. cit.,* I, 29.

9 *Ibid.,* pp. 35-36.

10 *Ibid.,* p. 33.

11 *Ibid.,* pp. 24-25. Blumhardt insisted on an adequate salary to care for his family, though he yielded to no one in his pursuit of piety.

12 *Ibid.,* p. 34.

13 *Ibid.,* p. 137. However, by 1852 there was a sharp drop in income from publications. See p. 186, note 109.

14 Henry W. Hulbert, "The Basel Mission," *The Missionary Review of the World,* I (New Series), No. 10 (Oct., 1888), pp. 742-48.

15 Not all the men who passed through the Basel Mission houses were artisans. One of them was Count Felician Zaremba, a Ph.D. and a state official in Russia who had been moved by a mighty conversion experience to sacrifice position, title, career, and family for Christ. He secured approval for the mission from Czar Alexander in an imperial audience. Zaremba became the ideal pioneer of the new Russian mission. One of the first Basel trainees to be sent to India was the very able young theologian Benedict La Roche, who had studied Sanskrit and other Oriental languages in Paris and Cambridge before entering the service of the Church Missionary Society in Calcutta. Tragically, he soon died in India (Schlatter, II, 1). Another well-trained man was Dr. Hermann Mögling, who had studied theology at Tübingen. He was part of the second contingent of missionaries for the Basel field on the west coast of India, arriving in 1836 (*ibid.,* 20). At about the same time, Dr. Hermann Gundert joined the staff of the Basel Mission in India. There were others too.

Chapter XII

1 Schlatter, *Geschichte der Basler Mission,* II, 154.

2 Paul Eppler, *Geschichte der Basler Mission, 1815-1899* (Basel: Missions-buchhandlung, 1900), pp. 171-72.

3 *Ibid.,* p. 172.

4 Schlatter, *op. cit.,* II, 155.

5 *Ibid.*

6 *Jahresbericht, Basler Mission,* 1847, pp. 60-61.

7 *Industrie-Commission, Jahresbericht,* 1853, p. 7.

8 Schlatter, *op. cit.,* II, 156.

9 *Industrie-Commission, Jahresbericht,* 1953, p. 7, tr. mine.

10 Schlatter, *op. cit.,* II, 158.

11 Wanner, *Die Basler Handelsgesellschaft,* p. 259.

12 Georg Plebst, "Die Anfänge und die Entwickelung der ostindischen Werkstätten," *Industrie-Commission, Jahresbericht,* 1869, pp. 14-17.

13 *Ibid.,* pp. 10ff.

14 Wanner, *op. cit.,* p. 260.

15 *Ibid.,* pp. 261-62.

16 *The Oxford English Dictionary* ascribes it to the Urdu language and to Persian derivation. *Webster's Third International Dictionary* says it comes through Hindi from a Persian word.

17 Wanner, *op. cit.,* pp. 263-64. See "The Origin of Khaki Claimed by Mangalore," *Madras Mail,* 29 October, 1903, and "Khaki, Its Inventor," April, 1904. However, this claim may be contested by some. *The Oxford English Dictionary* states that khaki was used for uniforms by the Guide Corps under Lumsden and Hodson in 1848, and by the troops in the Mutiny of 1857. John Haller first reached India in 1851. Apparently there were many khaki dyes in India by 1890. However, it may be quite correct that the Basel Mission industries were the means by which British commanders were stimulated to make wide use of khaki.

18 *Ibid.,* p. 264.

19 *Ibid.,* p. 265.

20 Eppler, *op. cit.,* p. 175.

21 Schlatter, *op. cit.,* II, 160.

22 *Ibid.,* p. 162.

23 Eppler, *op. cit.,* p. 176.

24 *Ibid.,* p. 177. See also Thomas Digel, "Dscheppu und seine Entwick-elung bis zur Errichtung der Dampf-Maschine," *Industrie-Commission, Jahres-bericht 1880/81.*

25 Schlatter, *op. cit.,* II, 163.

26 *Ibid.,* pp. 165-66.

27 C. J. Riggenbach, *Vertrauliche Mitteilungen über Handel und Industrie in der Basler Mission,* 1884, Archives of the Basel Mission Society, p. 6. One is reminded here of the Moravians who had pioneered the practice of firm prices in Europe in the previous century. See Herbert Hammer, *Abraham Dürninger, ein Herrnhuter Wirtschaftsmensch des achtzehnten Jahrhunderts* (Berlin: Furche, 1925), p. 33. This practice was carried out on a broad scale by Abraham Dürninger, the mercantile genius who developed the general store at Herrnhut into a many-sided enterprise doing business in many parts of the world (*ibid.,* p. 69).

28 Schlatter, *op. cit.,* p. 166.

29 *Missionary Review of the World,* IX, New York: Funk and Wagnalls, (July, 1896), p. 557.

30 F. Kühnle, *Die Arbeitsstätten der Basler Mission* (Basel: Missions-buchhandlung, 1895), p. 65.

31 Wanner, *op. cit.,* p. 282.

32 Digel, *op. cit.,* pp. 16-17.

33 *Ibid.*

34 Wilhelm Schlatter and Hermann Witschi, *Geschichte der Basler Mission 1914-1919,* p. 36.

35 *Ibid.*

Chapter XIII

1 See Wanner, *Die Basler Handelsgesellschaft,* pp. 516-530 for a complete necrology of the agents of the Basel Trading Society. However, it should be

noted that these brief and poignant notices do not include wives or children.

2 *Evangelisches Missions-Magazin* N.F. (1919), p. 153.

3 Eppler, *Geschichte der Basler Mission, 1815-1899,* pp. 85-88.

4 *Ibid.,* pp. 202-03. By bringing in the West Indians, Basel was emulating the Wesleyan Methodists. After all their early missionaries had died, a candidate volunteered whose heredity gave him a better chance of survival. This was the famed Thomas Birch Freeman (1809-1890), son of an African father and a white mother, who came to the deadly Gold Coast in 1838. Using his gardener's training, he began a model farm and introduced coffee, cinnamon, ginger, mangos, and olives (K. S. Latourette, *A History of the Expansion of Christianity,* V [New York: Harper & Bros., 1943] , 447).

5 Thus Friedrich Herzog of Riedlingen in Baden, friend of a young preaching missionary headed for Africa, volunteered to accompany him and help him as a lay brother, if only his trip were paid. Herzog was a carpenter and a mechanic. His passage, outfit, and tools were paid by the *Industrie-Commission (3. Jahresbericht der Industrie-Commission der Ev. Missionsgesellschaft in Basel vom Jahre 1855* [Basel: Bohnmeiers Buchdruckerei, 1856] , p. 18). See p. 21 for details on the cost of passage, tools, and outfit. Once on the field, he was to support himself. It was not until 1878 that the artisan missionaries in Africa were placed on the same financial basis as the ordained missionaries (Riggenbach, *Vertrauliche Mitteilungen,* p. 12).

6 Schlatter, *Geschichte der Basler Mission,* III, 190.

7 Wanner, *op. cit.,* p. 226. See also pp. 27-31.

8 W. Duisberg, *Industrie und Handel im Dienst der Basler Mission,* 2nd ed. See also Eppler, *op. cit.,* p. 204.

9 *Kommittee-Protokoll,* April 11, 1855. These minutes of the mission board are found in the Archives of the Basel Mission Society.

10 *3. Jahresbericht der Industrie-Commission der Ev. Missionsgesellschaft in Basel vom Jahre 1855,* p. 17.

11 For notarized documentary evidence see Gustav Adolf Wanner, *The First Cocoa Trees in Ghana 1858-68* (Basel: Basel Trading Company, 1962).

12 Wanner, *The First Cocoa Trees in Ghana 1858-68* (Basel: Basel Trading Company, 1962), p. 25.

13 *43. Bericht der Missions-Handlungs-Gesellschaft über das Geschäftsjahr 1902* (Basel: M. Werner-Riehm, 1903), p. 8. See also Wanner, *The First Cocoa Trees,* pp. 28-29.

14 Riggenbach, *op. cit.,* p. 10.

15 See Karl Hartenstein, *Anibue; Die 'Neue Zeit' auf der Goldküste und unsere Missionsaufgabe* (Stuttgart und Basel: Evangelischer Missionsverlag, 1932), pp. 23ff.

16 *52. Bericht der Missions-Handlungs-Gesellschaft über das Geschäftsjahr 1911* (Basel: Werner-Riehm, 1912), p. 10.

17 *The Missionary Review of the World,* XXXV (1912), pp. 389-90.

18 Duisberg, *op. cit.,* p. 20.

[19] Werner Kessler, "Die Alkoholfrage auf dem afrikanischen Missions-gebiet," *Die Alkoholfrage in der Religion,* IV, No. 3 (Berlin: Neuland-Verlag, 1931), p. 23.

[20] C. J. Riggenbach, *op. cit.,* p. 9.

[21] Schlatter, *op. cit.,* III, p. 193.

[22] This important document has been published in German translation by Fritz Raaflaub, "Ein wichtiges Dokument aus der Geschichte der Goldküste," *Evangelisches Missions-Magazin,* CII (February, 1958), pp. 28-40.

[23] London: Lutterworth Press, 1966.

Chapter XIV

[1] *Protokoll der Industrie-Commission der evangelischen Missions-Gesell-schaft in Basel,* I, 1846-1873, p. 1.

[2] *Jahresbericht der Industrie-Commission der Evangelischen Missionsgesell-schaft in Basel vom Jahre 1853,* pp. 3-4.

[3] *Ibid.*

[4] *Ibid.,* pp. 4-5.

[5] *Ibid.,* p. 5.

[6] *Jahresbericht 1852,* p. 9.

[7] By this time the Society periodicals were no longer showing the profits which they had in the palmy days of Blumhardt, netting only about 2,000 gulden per year.

[8] Eppler, *Geschichte der Basler Mission, 1815-1899,* p. 180.

[9] Wanner, *Die Basler Handelsgesellschaft,* pp. 34-38.

[10] *Statut der Missionshandlungsgesellschaft vom Mai 1859,* p. 2, Archives of the Basel Mission Society.

[11] Printed in *Verordnungen für die Basler Missionsstationen* (Verord-nungen, die Missionshandlungen betreffend), pp. 8-11, Archives of the Basel Mission Society, tr. mine.

[12] *Statuten der Missions-Handlungs-Gesellschaft 1869,* p. 11, Archives of the Basel Mission Society.

[13] Wanner, *op. cit.,* p. 60.

[14] *Beschlusz des Regierungsrates vom 22 Oktober 1879* (Staatsarchiv Basel-Stadt, Vereine und Gesellschaften F 10). See also *Bericht des Finanz-departements an den Regierungsrat vom 17 Oktober, 1879 (ibid.).*

[15] Eduard Preiswerk, *An die Mitglieder der Handlungskommission und der Kommittee der evang. Missionsgesellschaft in Basel, 1880,* p. 2. This was a confidential memorandum to the members of the trading commission and the mission board.

[16] *Ibid.,* p. 12.

[17] *Ibid.,* p. 3.

[18] *Ibid.,* p. 10.

19 *Ibid.,* p. 4.

20 *Statuten der Missionshandlungsgesellschaft, 1880,* p. 2.

21 *Ibid.*

22 *Statuten der Missions-Handlungs-Gesellschaft in Basel, Festgesetzt von der General-Versammlung am 9. Juni 1887,* p. 2, Archives of the Basel Mission Society.

23 *Ibid.,* pp. 2-3.

24 *Ibid.,* pp. 3-4.

25 *Statuten der Missions-Handlungs-Gesellschaft in Basel, Festgesetzt von der ausserordentlichen Generalversammlung vom 23. Februar 1912,* pp. 1-2, Archives of the Basel Mission Society.

26 Schlatter, *Geschichte der Basler Mission,* III, 192.

27 These figures were compiled on the basis of the annual reports by the *Industrie-Commission,* or *Missionshandlungsgesellschaft,* for the years in question. We do not have the totals for the years between 1859 and 1869. However, the mission's share of the profits after dividends to shareholders was between 6,000 and 18,000 francs. Of course, the mission received interest on its shares, as well. The table demonstrates how dramatically contributions to the mission rose after Eduard Preiswerk's reorganization of 1880.

28 *Bericht an die Missionshandlungs-Gesellschaft über das Geschäft im Jahre 1861* (Basel: Fritz Wassermann, 1862).

29 *54. Bericht an die Missions-Handlungs-Gesellschaft für das Geschäftsjahr 1913* (Basel: Werner-Riehm, 1914).

30 Thus, the *Handlungs-Commission* in Basel in 1867 resolved to use its influence to bring peace by opening a trading station at Akuambu. The mission treasury with a deficit of 160,000 francs could not remotely consider opening a station there. However, the *Handlungs-Commission* could afford it and, what is more, they could lay down the condition to the chief of Akuambu that he would have to keep the peace for a year as proof of good faith.

CHAPTER XV

1 Wanner, *Die Basler Handelsgesellschaft,* p. 48.

2 *Ibid.,* pp. 48-49.

3 C. J. Riggenbach, *Vertrauliche Mitteilungen,* p. 17.

4 *Ibid.*

5 *Ibid.*

6 *Ibid.,* p. 18, tr. mine.

7 *Ibid.*

8 *Ibid.,* p. 11.

9 *Ibid.,* p. 18.

10 *Ibid.,* p. 8.

11 *Siebenzigster Jahresbericht der Ev. Missionsgesellschaft der Evan-*

gelischen Missionsgesellschaft zu Basel (Basel: Missionsverwaltung, 1885), p. 2.

12 *Ibid.*

13 *Jahresbericht der Missions-Handlungs-Gesellschaft 1909,* par. 677.

14 *54. Bericht der Missions-Handlungs-Gesellschaft für das Geschäftsjahr 1913* (Basel: Werner-Riehm, 1914), pp. 9-10.

15 *52. Bericht der Missions-Handlungs-Gesellschaft über das Geschäftsjahr 1911.*

16 The new, well-paid contract workers represented a contrast to the former practice. The Archives of the Basel Mission Society, under copies of the correspondence of the *Handlungs-Commission,* contain a copy of a letter to "Herrn Sayler, bei Herrn Ph. Zimmermann in Heidelberg" dated 26 November 1867. It asks whether he would accept a call as a "Missionskaufmann." He is assured that mission merchants have the same status as the regular missionaries. They receive no regular salaries, but get annual allowances according to need, just as the other missionaries do. Therefore they are called to unlimited service "as long as the Lord makes it possible." He is informed: "Your tasks are those of a merchant; but you are at the same time a member of the station missionary conferences and of the presbyteries; you take part in the deliberations and in the congregational affairs, and have the liberty to preach and teach outside of the church in your free time."

17 *52. Bericht.* See note 15.

18 Friedrich Würz, "Die Basler Mission am Scheideweg," EMM (New Series), LXII (1918), p. 113.

19 *Ecumenical Missionary Conference, New York, 1900,* 2 vols. (New York: American Tract Society, 1900), II, 158.

20 Wilhelm Schlatter and Hermann Witschi, *Geschichte der Basler Mission 1914-1919,* p. 70.

21 *Statuten der Missions-Handlungs-Gesellschaft in Basel Festgesetzt von der auszerordentlichen Generalversammlung vom 20. November 1917,* art. (a), Archives of the Basel Mission Society. I follow the official English translation.

22 *Ibid.,* art. 12, p. 4.

23 Wilhelm Burckhardt, "Letter to Mr. Wilhelm Preiswerk-Imhoff" dated 4 July, 1928, at Basel. For some time previously, the Trading Company had not been using the word "mission" in its name.

24 *Statuten der Basler Handels-Gesellschaft AG in Basel (1961),* art. 17, p. 9.

25 Wanner, *op. cit.,* pp. 297-421.

26 In French Cameroun in 1921, in British Cameroun in 1923. Though they involved properties of relatively small value, these restitutions were important precedents.

27 T. S. Thomas, *The Basel Mission Trading Society and the Commonwealth Trust ... Memorandum XIV–1928-29* (Accra: Government Printing Office, 1929), p. 5. Thomas was Acting Governor at the time. Hereafter referred to as *Memorandum Thomas.*

28 *Ibid.,* p. 4.

29 *Ibid.,* pp. 7-8.

30 L. S. Amery in *Memorandum Thomas,* p. 14.

31 The Conference of British Missionary Societies, which Oldham had helped found soon after Edinburgh, together with the Foreign Missions Conference of North America organized the Emergency Committee of Cooperating Missions on April 14, 1918, to deal with pressing missionary concerns. John R. Mott was elected chairman, and Oldham and Kenneth Maclennan, Oldham's co-worker in the preparations for Edinburgh, were chosen as secretaries. The committee's functions were 1) to handle all questions of governmental relations in which the societies were jointly interested; 2) to consider means to provide for war-impaired missions; 3) to act as a clearing house and to harmonize the approach to major problems shared by all societies in the transition from war to peace. Oldham and Maclennan were secretaries of the Conference of British Missionary Societies, Maclennan serving on marginal time in addition to his war work for the British government (W. Richey Hogg, *Ecumenical Foundations; A History of the International Missionary Council and Its Nineteenth-Century Background* [New York: Harper and Brothers, 1952], p. 184).

32 *The Treaties of Peace 1919-1923,* 2 vols. (New York: Carnegie Endowment for International Peace, 1924), I, 261.

33 Schlatter and Witschi, *op. cit.,* p. 295.

34 L. S. Amery, *Dispatch to the Officer Administering the Affairs of the Gold Coast. Gold Coast No. 657. Dated 31st July, 1928, Downing Street, London. Memorandum XIV. The Basel Mission Trading Society and the Commonwealth Trust,* p. 12.

35 *Ibid.*

36 *Ibid.,* p. 13.

37 Wanner, *op. cit.,* p. 320.

38 *Ibid.*

39 *Statuten . . . 1917,* p. 4, tr. mine.

40 Wanner, *op. cit.,* p. 333.

41 "Basle Trading Co.," *Parliamentary Debates, House of Lords,* 22 February 1928, LXX, col. 225.

42 *Ibid.,* col. 224.

43 *Ibid.,* 9 May 1928, col. 1066.

44 This was pointed out by Lord Lovat of the Colonial Office in the course of debate in the House of Lords on May 9, 1928 (*ibid.,* col. 1068). One of the speakers, Lord Olivier, objected to paying £55,000 to the Commonwealth Trust Ltd.: "Talk about State Socialism, I would very much rather take over the whole education of the natives of Cape Colony and the Gold Coast than I would give a fund or an endowment to a commercial company in order that they might make profits out of which they can provide for the education of the natives. It is a shocking principle" (*ibid.,* col. 1043). Earl Buxton pitied the people of the Colony, "notably the traders, because they will have to pay

the money both to the Basel Trading Company and to the Commonwealth Trust and they will be saddled with two rival traders whom they will be subsidising out of their own pockets" (*ibid.*, col. 1049). Of course, some of those people and traders had voted for the illegal seizure in the first place.

45 *Parliamentary Debates, House of Commons,* 12 March 1928, CCXIV, No. 25, col. 1491.

46 *The Commonwealth Education and Welfare Trust 1919-1961.* Mimeographed publication issued by the Commonwealth Education and Welfare Trust at its office at 11 Lowfield Road, London W. 3, November 1961, pp. 5-6.

47 *Memorandum Thomas,* p. 16.

48 *Ibid.*

49 "Commonwealth Trust Limited," *Parliamentary Debates, House of Commons,* CCXIV, No. 25, 12 March 1928, col. 1489-1493. At one point the trading losses of the Commonwealth Trust, Ltd. exceeded £ 350,000. And this for a firm capitalized at only £ 60,000, later £ 100,000! By 1927, however, the financial position of the Trust had shown substantial improvement (*ibid.,* col. 1491). Then the shareholders were bold enough to appropriate a first sum of £ 2,500 to the trustees for welfare and educational purposes, but they did it in "anticipation of future surplus profits" (*ibid.,* col. 1489).

50 These figures are based on annual reports of the Basel Trading Company. The company did not make contributions every year during that decade.

51 *The Commonwealth Education and Welfare Trust 1919-1961,* p. 15.

52 *Ibid.,* p. 17.

53 *Parliamentary Debates, House of Lords,* 11 July 1934, XCIII, No. 78, col. 460.

54 Wanner, *op. cit.,* p. 418.

55 *Memorandum Thomas,* p. 14.

56 Frank Short, "Letter to Mr. William Preiswerk," dated 12 January, 1965, at Edinburgh House, London.

57 It is true that authorities in England had paved the way by expelling all missionaries of the Basel Mission Society and all employees of the Basel Trading Company.

58 This would have been to penalize the public-spirited citizens and friends of missions who had formed the Commonwealth Trust Ltd. and invested £ 60,000 (later £ 100,000) in it. As we have seen above, at one point their operations were running at a loss of £ 350,000. Liquidation at that point would have been a great injustice to shareholders, creditors, and employees.

59 *Parliamentary Debates, House of Lords,* 9 May 1928, col. 1053. One is struck by the British sense of justice and fair play not only to the Basel Trading Company but also to the Commonwealth Trust Ltd.

60 *Ibid.,* col. 1056.

61 *Ibid.,* col. 1065. This concern is also clearly apparent from the debate in

the House of Lords on 9 May 1928. A number of members of the House were also directors or former directors of the Commonwealth Trust Ltd.

62 Frank Short, "Letter to Mr. William Preiswerk." This illustrates once more how diverging interests and dynamics were at work moving the company and the mission apart.

63 At a wartime conference on German missions in Halle, Oct. 7 and 8, 1914, the offer of British missionary leaders to gather a special offering for fields of Continental mission societies cut off from their headquarters, was presented. There was no doubt in the minds of German missionary leaders that the whole plan originated from the purest fraternal feelings. However, it was declined "because of the serious injustice between the British and the German people and because the gift would represent a gift from the British people," EMM, LVIII (1914), 466, tr. mine.

64 Friedrich Würz, "Die Basler Mission am Scheideweg," EMM, LXII (1918), 129. This article is most instructive about the painful dilemma of the Basel Mission during the troubled years of World War I. In a letter dated 28 January 1918 at Bern, the British Legation informed Basel that both the Mission Society and the Trading Company were according to the decision of H. M. Government to be excluded from British territory because they were "to all intents and purposes" German organizations (ibid., p. 128). It is another illustration of the futility of seeking to maintain the supranational character of missions at a time of widespread international conflict.

65 In addition, 200 out of its total of 1000 shares, the shares that once belonged to the Basel Mission Society, now belong to a special foundation, the Paulus-Fond. Its proceeds are distributed by a special set of trustees, who, however, are no longer appointed by the Basel Mission Society. Even the most tenuous organizational ties have been severed.

66 The Rev. Paul Volz, then missionary in Nigeria, in a private conversation with the author in early 1964.

Chapter XVI

1 C. J. Riggenbach, Vertrauliche Mitteilungen über Handel und Industrie in der Basler Mission, p. 15. The replies are made in the name of the whole mission board.

2 Ibid.

3 Michael Hollis, Paternalism and the Church: A Study of South Indian Church History (London: Oxford University Press, 1962), p. 60.

4 Riggenbach, op. cit., p. 16.

5 L. J. Frohnmeyer, "The Basel Industrial Missions in India," Ecumenical Missionary Conference, New York, 1900. Report of the Ecumenical Conference on Foreign Missions, Held in Carnegie Hall and Neighboring Churches, April 21 to May 1, II, 157.

6 Ibid., p. 160.

7 Ibid., p. 162.

8 Schlatter, Geschichte der Basler Mission, II, 163.

9 Peter Reinhold Grundmann, *Missions-Studien und Kritiken* (Gütersloh: C. Bertelsmann, 1894), pp. 54-55, tr. mine.

10 H. Huizinga, *Our Interest as a Mission in Industrial Work for Our Telugu Boys* (Madras: M. E. Press, 1903), pp. 4-5.

11 See Miss Hesse, "Die Allgemeine Missions-Conferenz zu Allahabad in December, 1872. 3. Die Stellung der Mission gegenüber den aüsseren Lebensverhältnissen ihrer Bekehrten," EMM, XVIII (New Series, 1874), 177-195. See esp. p. 187.

12 Carl Christian Reindorf, *History of the Gold Coast and Asante* (Basel: Missionsbuchhandlung, 1895), pp. 227-228. Notwithstanding his German name, Reindorf was an African.

13 The Rev. T. A. Beetham, twenty years a missionary in Ghana (1929-1949) and now Africa secretary of the Conference of British Missionary Societies, in conversation with the writer, October 14, 1964, at Concordia Seminary, St. Louis, Mo. The United Africa Co. among others also follows high standards, but Africans have recognized that Basel set the tone.

14 Udipi Municipal Council, *Civic Address Presented to Rev. J. Rossel, President, Ev. Missionary Soc., Basel,* Udipi, South Kanara, Jan. 30, 1964.

15 Karl Barth, born in Basel in 1886 as son of a professor of New Testament at the University, returned to the same school as professor of systematic theology in 1935. The University is only a five- or ten-minute walk from the *Missionshaus;* and the modern five-story headquarters of the Basel Trading Company is right across the street from the university building.

16 In a conversation with the writer, January 31, 1967, at the Basel *Missionshaus,* Basel, Switzerland.

17 L. J. Frohnmeyer, "Die Basler Mission in Indien und der Krieg," EMM, LXII (1918), 276.

18 After employees were sent overseas on a contract basis rather than with missionary status, this training approached the vanishing point. Since the separation of Trading Company and Mission in World War I, the Mission has had no opportunity to give such training. But the Company always made every effort to recruit people with a Christian Protestant background.

19 *A Theology of the Laity* (Philadelphia: Westminster, 1958).

20 Eppler, *op. cit.,* p. 181.

21 Schlatter, *op. cit.,* I, 395.

22 Riggenbach, *op. cit.,* p. 15.

23 Thus W. Duisberg, *Industrie und Handel im Dienst der Basler Mission.* The probable date is 1907. The words of Eduard Preiswerk, former longtime president, on the "how" of recruitment are quoted: "We send out all the young merchants whom God sends us. We pray Him to send us the right people." No distinction was made in the recruitment of ordained and lay brethren. Duisberg makes his appeal to Christian youth organizations as the nurseries of merchants and artisans in plenty whom God could call into the mission field. "If true mission mindedness and proper acquaintance with missions to the heathen is planted in all such societies in Germany and

Switzerland, then we shall surely never lack sufficient co-workers in the missions" (p. 48, tr. mine). The mission board even promised to make it possible for recruits with financial responsibilities to their families who had the inner call to missions, to discharge such responsibilities (*ibid.*).

24 See Duisberg, *Industrie und Handel.*

25 See Friedrich Würz, EMM, New Series, LXII (1918), 130.

Chapter XVII

1 There have been notable exceptions to this rule. Some clergymen with native gifts or commercial background have scored outstanding success in business. When theological motivation and orientation are added to talent and experience the results can be good. But to avoid disadvantage to the clergyman's primary role, it is generally best if lay people manage economic activities.

2 Peter G. Batchelor and Harry R. Boer, *Theology and Rural Development in Africa* (Grand Rapids, Michigan: William B. Eerdmans Publishing Company, 1966), p. 13.

3 See Frantz Fanon, *The Wretched of the Earth,* tr. from the French (New York: Grove Press, 1968). Though Fanon is fiercely Marxist, he speaks for much wider circles in Africa, Asia, and Latin America when he expresses bitter resentment of economic and therefore also cultural exploitation by the West.

4 Walter Freytag, "Geld und Geist in der Werdenden Kirche," *Reden und Aufsätze,* 2 vols. (München: Chr. Kaiser Verlag, 1961), I, 269.

5 "After the Monks-What?" *The Springfielder,* XXXI, No. 3 (Autumn 1967), pp. 3-21.

6 The interested reader is referred to the statistics on church giving published in the *Yearbook of American Churches* published annually by the National Council of the Churches of Christ in the U.S.A., 475 Riverside Drive, New York 27, New York.

7 Alfred Balk, *The Religion Business* (Richmond, Va.: John Knox Press, 1968), p. 26.

Bibliography

A. The Moravians

Beyreuther, Erich. *Nikolaus Ludwig von Zinzendorf.* Reinbeck bei Hamburg: Rowohlt, 1965.

–––. *Zinzendorf.* 3 vols. Marburg a.d. Lahn: Francke, 1957-61.

Buchner, C. *Acht Monate in Südafrika: Schilderung der dortigen Mission der Brüdergemeine.* Gütersloh: C. Bertelsmann, 1894.

Büdingsche Sammlung einiger in die Kirchen-Historie Einschlagender Sonderlich neuerer Schriften. Büdingen: Joh. Chr. Stöhr, 1742.

Calker, E. van. *Die Grant-Stationen in Süd-Afrika.* Hefte zur Missions-Kunde Nr. 5. Herrnhut: Missionsbuchhandlung, 1909.

Erbe, Helmuth. *Bethlehem, Pa., Eine kommunistische Herrnhuter Kolonie des 18. Jahrhunderts.* Stuttgart: Ausland und Heimat Verlags-Hg., 1929.

Gollin, Gillian Lindt. *Moravians in Two Worlds: A Study of Changing Communities.* New York: Columbia University, 1967.

Gray, Elma E. *Wilderness Christians: The Moravian Missions to the Delaware Indians.* Ithaca, New York: Cornell University, 1956.

Gysin, Alfred. *Mission im Heimatland der Eskimos.* Hamburg: Ludwig Appel, 1966.

Hamilton, J. Taylor, and Kenneth G. Hamilton. *History of the Moravian Church: The Renewed Unitas Fratrum, 1722-1957.* Bethlehem, Pa.: Moravian Church in America, 1967.

Hammer, Herbert. *Abraham Dürninger: Ein Herrnhuter Wirtschaftsmensch des achtzehnten Jahrhunderts.* Berlin: Furche, 1925.

Helman, Albert. *Business, Mission and Meditation: The Romance of a Two Hundred Year Old Suriname Company.* Paramaribo: C. Kersten, 1968.

Hinchcliff, Peter. *The Church in South Africa.* London: SPCK, 1968.

Krüger, Bernhard. *The Pear Tree Blossoms: A History of the Moravian Mission Stations in South Africa 1737-1869.* Genadendal, South Africa: Genadendal Printing Works, 1967.

Langton, Edward. *History of the Moravian Church.* London: Moravian Publications Office, 1895.

Levering, Joseph Mortimer. *The History of Bethlehem 1741-1892.* 3 vols. Bethlehem, Pa.: Times Publishing Co., 1903.

Lord, E. *A Compendious History of the Principal Protestant Missions to the Heathen.* Boston: Samuel T. Armstrong, 1813.

Mortimer, Benjamin. *Diary of the Indian Congregation at Goshen on the River Muskingum from 1st May to 31st October, 1800.*

–––. *Diary of the Indian Congregation at Goshen on the Muskingum from June 1, 1801, to May 31, 1802.*

–––. *Protokoll der Missions-Conferenz, gehalten in Gosen am Muskingum, vom 10ten bis zum 21ten Oct., 1803,* Moravian Archives, Bethlehem, Pa.

Müller, Karl. *200 Jahre Brüdermission,* vol. I, *Das erste Jahrhundert.* Herrnhut: Missionsbuchhandlung, 1931.

Peacock, F. W. "The Moravian Mission in Labrador," *Canadian Geographic Journal,* LX, May 1960, 185.

Schneider, H. G. *Die Ermordung Erhardts und seiner Genossen; Aus der Vorgeschichte der Labradormission.* Hefte zur Missionskunde Nr. 11. Herrnhut: Missionsbuchhandlung, 1913.

Schulze, Adolf. *200 Jahre Brüdermission,* II, *Das Zweite Jahrhundert.* Herrnhut: Missionsbuchhandlung, 1932.

Schweinitz, Edmund de. *The Life and Times of David Zeisberger.* Philadelphia: Lippincott, 1870.

Sessler, Jacob John. *Communal Pietism among Early American Moravians.* New York: Holt, 1933.

Spangenberg, August Gottlieb. *Von der Arbeit der evangelischen Brüder unter den Heiden.* Barby: Christian Friedrich Laux, 1782.

Stähelin, F. *Die Mission der Brüdergemeine in Suriname und Berbice im achtzehnten Jahrhundert.* Herrnhut: Verein für Brüdergeschichte und Paramaribo, C. Kersten, n.d. 3 vols. in 6 parts.

Thompson, Augustus C. *Moravian Missions.* New York: Scribner's, 1882.

Uttendörfer, Otto. *Alt-Herrnhut: Wirtschaftsgeschichte und Religions-soziologie Herrnhuts während der ersten zwanzig Jahre (1722-1742).* Herrnhut: Missionsbuchhandlung, 1925.

–––. *Die wichtigsten Missionsinstruktionen Zinzendorfs.* Hefte zur Missionskunde Nr. 12. Herrnhut: Missionsbuchhandlung, 1913.

Wagner, Hans. *Abraham Dürninger & Co. 1747-1939.* 2nd ed. Herrnhut: Abraham Dürninger-Stiftung, 1940.

Weinlick, John R. *Count Zinzendorf.* Nashville: Abingdon, 1956.

Zeisberger, David. *Diary of Goschgoschünk and Lawunakhanek, Feb. 25-Sept. 7, 1769.* Moravian Archives, Bethlehem, Pa.

B. The Basel Mission Trading Company

Amery, L. S. *Dispatch to the Officer Administering the Affairs of the Gold Coast. Gold Coast No. 657. Dated 31st July, 1928, Downing Street, London – Memorandum XIV. The Basel Mission Trading Society and the Commonwealth Trust.* Accra: Government Printing Office, 1928.

Berichte der Missions-Handlungs-Gesellschaft. Archives of the Basel Mission Society.

Debrunner, Hans W. *A History of Christianity in Ghana.* Accra: Waterville, 1967.

Digel, Thomas. "Dscheppu und seine Entwickelung bis zur Errichtung der Dampf-Maschine," *Industrie-Commission Jahresbericht 1880/81.* Basel: Ferd. Riehm, 1882.

Duisberg, W. *Industrie und Handel im Dienst der Basler Mission.* 2nd ed. Basel: Missionsbuchhandlung, n.d.

"Ein Dankfest der Missionsweberei in Kannanur," *Heidenbote,* LI, Basel: 1878.

Eppler, Paul. *Geschichte der Basler Mission, 1815-1899.* Basel: Missionsbuchhandlung, 1900.

Frohnmeyer, L. J. "The Basel Industrial Missions in India," *Ecumenical Missionary Conference, New York, 1900. Report of the Ecumenical Conference on Foreign Missions, Held in Carnegie Hall and Neighboring Churches, April 21 to May 1.* 2 vols. New York: American Tract Society; London: Religious Tract Society, 1900.

–––. "Die Basler Mission in Indien und der Krieg," *Evangelisches Missions-Magazin,* LXIII, 1918.

Grundmann, Peter Reinhold. *Missions-Studien und Kritiken.* Gütersloh: C. Bertelsmann, 1894.

Harris, John H. *Dawn in Darkest Africa.* London: Smith, Elder, 1912.

Jahresberichte der Evangelischen Missionsgesellschaft zu Basel.

Jahresberichte der Industrie-Commission der Evangelischen Missionsgesellschaft in Basel. Basel Mission Society Archives.

Kühnle, F. *Die Arbeitsstätten der Basler Mission.* Basel: Missionsbuchhandlung, 1895.

Plebst, Georg. "Die Anfänge und Entwickelung der ostindischen Werkstätten," *Industrie-Commission Jahresbericht 1869.* Basel Mission Society Archives.

Preiswerk, Eduard. *An die Mitglieder der Handlungskommission und der Kommittee der evang. Missionsgesellschaft in Basel, 1880.* Basel Mission Society Archives. This was a confidential memorandum to the members of the trading commission and the mission board.

Protokoll der Industrie-Commission der evangelischen Missions-Gesellschaft in Basel, vol. I, 1846-1873. Basel Mission Society Archives. Basel, Switzerland.

Reindorf, Carl Christian. *History of the Gold Coast and Asante.* Basel: Missionsbuchhandlung, 1895.

Riggenbach, C. J. *Vertrauliche Mitteilungen über Handel und Industrie in der Basler Mission* 1884. Basel Mission Society Archives.

Schlatter, Wilhelm. *Geschichte der Basler Mission.* 3 vols. Basel: Missionsbuchhandlung, 1916.

Schlatter, Wilhelm and Hermann Witschi. *Geschichte der Basler Mission 1914-1919.* Nach einem Manuskript von Wilhelm Schlatter+ bearbeitet von Hermann Witschi. Basel: Basileia Verlag, 1965.

Statuten der Basler Handels-Gesellschaft AG in Basel.

Statuten der Missionshandlungsgesellschaft. Basel Mission Society Archives.

Thomas, T. S. *The Basel Mission Trading Society and the Commonwealth Trust . . . Memorandum XIV—1928-29.* Accra: Government Printing Office, 1928.

Wanner, Gustav Adolf. *Die Basler Handelsgesellschaft.* Basel: Basel Handels-Gesellschaft, 1959.

———. *The First Cocoa Trees in Ghana 1858-68.* Basel: Basel Trading Company, 1962.

"Wie wir Kaufleute mit den Missionaren zusammen arbeiten," *Aus der Werkstatt des Missionars. Vorträge, Ansprachen und Predigt auf der 5. allgemeinen studentischen Missionskonferenz vom 18. — 22. April 1913 in Halle a.S. gehalten.* Berlin-Lichterfelde: Verlag des Studentenbundes für Mission, 1913.

Würz, Friedrich. "Die Basler Mission am Scheideweg," *Evangelisches Missions-Magazin,* New Series, LXII, 1918.

Index

Abraham Dürninger Foundation 146
Accra 94, 122
Africa 85, 93ff., 118, 121, 122, 124, 162, 170
agriculture 26, 54, 66, 67, 73, 84, 85
Akuambu 164
Alaska 73, 158
alcohol 50, 60, 137
Algiers 28
Allahabad 128
Alpirsbach 80
Altona 96
America 45, 112
American Province, North 158
Amery, L. S. 119, 166
Amish 28
Amity 45, 46
Amsterdam 60, 66
Anglican mission 69
Antarctica 130
Antigua 95
Arakullu 126
Arakullu Tiling Establishment 90
Arawak Indians 51
Aristotle 146
Armenian clergy 82
artisans 26, 29, 32, 72-74, 80, 83, 87, 91, 92, 95
Asia 170
Augsburg 80
Augsburg Confession 159

Bad Boll 146

Baden 162
Balk, Alfred 170
Balmatha 88, 89
Bantus 68
Barth, Karl 129, 169
Basel: city of 14, 79-81, 86, 96, 114, 130, 156, 159, 164, 169; mission board in 89, 159, 160, 162, 168, 169; mission institute in 81; pietistic spirit of 79, 113, 123
Basel Mission Society; Basel Society; Basel mission

economic failures in: arrowroot 86; clocks 86; cocoanut oil 86; farming 84, 85; silk culture 86; watchmaking 86

economic successes of: agriculture 84, 85; bookbinding 86, 87; building 90; carpentry 87; cinnamon 162; cocoa 85, 97, 98, 130; coffee 95, 97, 162; cotton 97, 108; credit union 88, 89, 137; department stores 122; farming 162; ginger 162; health insurance 88, 137; home ownership 137; hosiery factory 129; mangoes 95, 162; mechanical workshops 109, 129; metal working 95; mission publications 81, 131; motor agency 98; olives 162; oranges 95; palm nuts 97, 98; pottery 89; publishing 81, 82, 86, 129; rice 85; river steamer 97; rubber 97; shoemaking 80, 81, 95; shops 80, 96; straw plaiting 95; tile making 87, 89-91, 126, 129, 130, 138; tobacco 95; trade 95-97, 103, 130; trucks 98; weaving 86-91, 127, 129, 130, 138; woodworking 87, 95

history of 80, 93, 101, 159, 160, 161, 163, 167, 168, 169

problems of: climate 93, 94; conflict between business and mission 87, 108, 109, 111, 131, 135; dealings with Government 104, 112ff., 131, 140; dealings with Scots 82; laziness 84; relation between missionary and artisan 130, 132, 135, 136

purpose of 80, 81, 95, 99, 102, 106, 138, 139

successes of: training of apprentices 95, 106, 122; uniting business with mission 121, 122, 126, 127, 131, 134

tensions between mission and economics 87, 108, 109

Basel *Missionshaus* 130

Basel Mission Trading Company 14, 64, 97-99, 103, 110, 111, 114, 115, 118, 120-122

Basel Mission Trading Society 113-115, 132

Basel Trading Company 94, 116-122, 128, 131, 167, 168, 169

Basel Trading Company Ltd. 111, 112

Basel Trading Society 121, 161

Batchelor, Peter G. 170

Baudert, S. 154

Baumann, Jacob 89

Bavianskloof 66, 67

Bayonne 56

Beaver, R. Pierce 42, 150, 151

Beck, Siegfried 60, 155

Beetham, T. A. 169

Berbice 52, 53, 57, 73

Bergen 18

Berlin 80

Berlin Mission Society 14

Bern 56, 168

Berthelsdorf 17

Bethel 158

Bethlehem 147, 148, 151, 152, 158

Bethlehem Pact 25-29, 71

Beyreuther, Erich 26, 143, 146, 147, 149, 150

Bieler, Andre 145

Bilanzen 146

Bilbao 56

Blanke, Fritz 144

Blumhardt, Christian Gottlieb 81, 160, 163

Board of Foreign Missions of the Moravian Church in America, Inc. 158

Boer, Harry R. 170

Boers 66

Bohemia 51, 66

Bormeister 80

Boston 153

Bradford 146

Bremerhaven 97

Brethren Commercial Society 53

British Cameroun 165

British Moravian Church 157

Brock, Peter 145

Brot für die Welt 122

Buchner, C. 159

Burckhardt, Wilhelm 165

Burckhardt-Forcart, Daniel 96

Bürg 81

Buxton, Earl 166

Cadiz 56

Calcutta 160

Calicut 90, 91

California 72, 104

Calvin, John 145

Cambridge 160

Cameroun 96, 97, 112, 122

Cannes 79

Cape Colony 166

Cape of Good Hope 67-69

Capetown 66

Carey, William 16, 158

Carson, Lord 119

"Casa Alemana" 62

Ceylon 28
Chelcicky, Peter 145
Christian VI 18
Christian Brothers 104
"Christian Commerce" 128, 138
Christiansborg 93-97, 99, 128
Christiansbrunn 25
Church Missionary Society 80, 160
"Civilization Fund" 151
C. Kersten and Co. 56-61, 63-65, 73, 104, 154, 155
colonization 32, 139
Commonwealth Trust Limited 112, 115, 117-120, 166, 167
Concordia Seminary 169
Conference of British Missionary Societies 166, 169
consilium abeundi 148
Copenhagen 17-19
credit system 47-50
credit unions 88, 89, 137
Curacao 68
Currie, Archibald 63
Czar Alexander 160

Daele, J. V. 150
Danish-Halle mission 14, 16, 17
Dehne 51, 52
De Kraker, J. 155
Delaware nation 42
De Schweinitz, Edmund 25, 145, 147, 149, 151, 152
Deutsche Christentumsgesellschaft 80, 81
Dharwar 122
Digel, Thomas 161
Dober, Leonhard 18, 31
Dreher 80
"drei Stände" 157
Duisberg, W. 162, 169, 170
Dürninger, Abraham 22-24, 26, 56, 74, 146, 154, 161
Dürr, Wilhelm 80

economic activities and mission 13, 14, 18, 124-142: benefits of 24, 30, 47, 51, 53, 55, 58, 64, 65, 67, 72, 74, 80, 81, 83, 96, 98, 99, 102, 103, 106, 107, 111, 126, 127, 134, 138, 139, 142; distinguished, but not separate 63, 73, 75, 109, 131, 135; separation of 48, 49, 59, 62, 92, 108, 111, 118, 131, 132; tensions of 23, 87, 108, 110
ecumenical activities 61, 121, 133, 134, 142
Ecumenical Missionary Conference 16
Edinburgh 166
Egede, Hans 14, 18
Egypt 28
Eliot, John 41, 151
Emergency Committee of Cooperating Missions 166
England 20, 24, 43, 45, 100, 116, 159, 167
Episcopal 158
Eppler, Paul 101, 160, 161, 162, 163, 169
Erbe, Helmuth 147, 159
Erhardt, John Christian 43
Eskimo 43-45, 47-50, 153, 158
Executive Service Corps 140

factory system 22, 91, 138
Fanon, Frantz 170
Fernando Po 97
Feuchter 126
Fluntern 80
Foreign Missions Conference of North America 166
Foreign Mission Society of the Moravian Church, South 158
Francke, August Hermann 17, 18, 33, 144
fratres legis Christi 17
Freeman, Thomas Birch 162
French Cameroun 165
Freytag, Walter 170
Friedenshütten 39, 40
Friedensthal 25
Frohmeyer, L. J. 168
Frohnmeyer, L. F. 169
Fulneck 146

Gandhi 92
Gapp, S. H. 153, 154, 156
Genadendal 67; *see also* Gnadenthal

"General Economy" 25-29, 71
General Missions Conference 128
General Synod 58, 59, 62, 72
gens aeterna 19
Georgia 51
Germany 52, 80, 89, 114, 146, 149, 158, 169
Gersdorf, Henriette Catherine von 17
Ghana 96-98, 115, 118, 122, 169
Gnadenfrei 74
Gnadenhütten 40, 41, 43, 73, 152
Gnadenthal 25; see also Genadendal
Gold Coast 28, 93-95, 97, 99, 100, 108, 110, 112-114, 116, 117, 119, 128, 162, 166
Gold Coast Legislative Council 117
Gollin, Gillian Lindt 24, 26, 29, 30, 143, 145, 146, 147, 148, 149
Goshen 40
Gotha 156
Gray, Elma E. 148, 152, 158
Great Britain 111, 112, 119
Greece 131
Greenland 14, 18, 27, 38, 45, 48, 75
Grundmann, Peter Reinhold 169
Guide Corps 161
Gundert, Hermann 160
Gysin, Alfred 152, 153

Halle 18, 19, 22, 26, 33, 144, 168
Haller, John 87, 88, 161
Hallesche Nachrichten 33
Halter, Niklaus 104
Hamburg 60, 98
Hamilton, J. Taylor 144, 150, 153, 155
Hamilton, Kenneth G. 144, 150, 153, 155
Hammer, Herbert 24, 146, 154, 161
Handlung der Missionsanstalt der Evangelischen Brüder-Unität 62
Handlungs-Commission 164, 165
Harlem 56
Harmony 46, 48
Hartenstein, Karl 129, 162
Haven, Jens 44, 45
health insurance 88, 137
Hebich, Samuel 123

Hebich Technical Training School 123
Hebron 48
Heidelberg 165
Heidelberg Catechism 159
Heidenbote 81
Heidendiakonie 53
Helman, Albert 64, 65, 153, 154, 155
Henry, Bishop 79
Herrnhut 17, 19, 20, 22, 24, 26, 27, 29, 31, 38, 43, 51, 53, 55, 56, 59, 62, 66, 74, 80, 133, 137, 154, 156, 161
Herzog, Friedrich 162
Hesse 169
Hilfswerk der Evangelischen Kirchen der Schweiz 122
Hindi 160
Hitler 155
Hodson 161
Hoffmann, Wilhelm 85, 94
Hogg, W. Richey 166
Holland 51, 61, 156
Hollis, Michael 168
Holstein 144
home ownership program 88, 137
Hottentots 66-69, 156
House of Commons 119
House of Lords 116, 118, 119, 166, 167
Hromadka, Josef L. 27
Huber 148
Hudson Bay Company 47, 49, 50
Huizenga, H. 169
Hulbert, Henry W. 160
Humphrey, Hubert 141
Hüningen 79
Hus, John 17
Hutberg 17
Hüttinger, Karl 90
Hutterites 28
Hutton, J. E. 149

Ignatius 40
India 14, 16, 17, 83ff., 95, 102, 103, 109, 112, 116, 117ff., 124, 129, 130, 158, 160, 161

Industrial Revolution 74, 91
Industrie-Commission 164
Ireland 119
Irion, Johann Ludwig 80

Jackson, Sheldon 158
Jamaica 57, 95
Jänicke, Johannes 80
Japan 85, 137
Jefferson, Thomas 40
Jena 22
Jeppoo 126
Jerusalem 72
Jesuits 33, 39, 68, 112
Jesus Christ 64, 77, 129, 135, 140, 142, 156, 160
Jews 28, 42
Josenhans, G. 110
Josenhans, Joseph 96, 101, 108
Joshua, Luke 87
Jutland 75

Kandahar 88
Karabagh 82
Katpadi 122
Kellaway, William 153
Kellenbenz, Hermann 144
Kersten, Christoph 154
Kessler, Werner 163
khaki 88, 161
Khoznikodi 90
Knecht, Peter 80
Koi-koin, Khoikhoi 68
Kraemer, Hendrik 130
Kraker, Jozias de 63
Kühnle 161
Kurland 80
Kyimbila 68

Labrador 22, 36, 43-50, 53, 59, 72, 97, 153, 158
Labrador Ship Company 45
Langton, Edward 144, 146
Lapland 158
La Roche, Benedict 160
Larsen, Jens 144
Larsen, Kay 144
Latin America 45, 170

Latourette, K. S. 162
Laurvig, Count Ferdinand Danneskjold 18
Lawaetz, Herman Carl 150
laymen 53, 54, 130, 136
Laymen's Missionary Movement 116
Leeds 146
Leipzig Mission Society 14
Lettres Edifiantes 33
Levering, Joseph Mortimer 147
Liberia 122
Lichtveld, Lou 153
Linder, Karl 47
liquor 39, 40, 99, 113, 115
Lisbon 56
Livorno 56
London 21, 45-47, 99, 144, 167
London Association in Aid of the Mission of the United Brethren 158
London Missionary Society 80, 159
Long, Walter 115
Lord, E. 149
Losungen 149
Lovat, Lord 166
Luklin, Tommy 86
Lumsden 161
Luther, Martin 55, 145, 157
Lutterodt 94

Maclennan, Kenneth 115, 116, 166
Madras 86, 88, 122, 127
Madras Mail 86
Magazin 81
Magdalena 66
Mahoning River 151, 152
Mahratta 85
Malabar 83, 84, 90, 137
Mangalore 84, 85, 87-90, 92, 102, 122, 123
Marriage Promotion Fund 57
Massachusetts 41, 153
Mayhews 151
medical mission 139
Meniolagomekah 151
Merian, Christoph 106
Methodists 100, 158
Metz, J. F. 86
Mexico 39

Michigan 41

militia Christi 34, 149

Mission Committee 103

Mission Institute 80, 81

Mission Land Bill 69

Missionsanstalt der Evangelischen Brüder-Unität 59, 62

Missionshandlungsgesellschaft 164

Missionshaus 169

Mission Society 105, 106, 111, 114, 115, 122

Mission Stations Act 69

Mission Trading Company 103-105, 107-109, 111

Missouri 169

Mögling, Hermann 160

Mohr, Arnold 97

Molner, Enrico C. S. 149

Moravia 51

Moravians (*see also* Unitas Fratrum; Unity; *fratres legis Christi;* Moravian Mission) 13-79, 95, 130, 133-142

communalism of: economy 19, 27, 29, 35, 36; labor 25; life 26-28, 34, 38, 145, 158; for communalism 26; against communalism 21, 38; communalism ended 27

economic successes of: agriculture 25, 26, 39, 60, 67; apothecary shop 20, 21; automobile dealership 60; bakery 52, 53, 56, 60; baskets 40; beer 20, 25, 27, 60; bicycle and motorcycle department 60; blacksmith 27, 35, 60, 67; bookstore 56; bricklaying 35, 53; building business 57; butter 40; canoes 40; carpentry 31, 35, 66, 68; cattle 40, 52; chairs 40; coffee 68; corn 40; credit union 29, 137; cutlery 67; department store 56, 60, 146; drapery goods 60; earth-moving machinery 60; fish 38, 47; flax 20; furs 47, 49; gardens 40; general store 21, 22, 53; health insurance 137; hogs 40; home ownership 137; hotel 60, 146; hunting 38; industry 67, 68; insurance department 60; linen 23, 25, 52-54, 56, 58, 74, 146; lunch-room 60; maple sugar 40; mats 40; mattress factory 60; oil 47; orchards 40; parking garage 60; pottery 25; poultry 40; reindeer herding 73, 158; salt 20; sawmill 73; sheep ranch 68; ships 22; shipping 153, 154; shoemaking 32, 35, 53, 60, 73; shoe-shining 25; sieves 40; soft drinks 60; sugar 68; tailor 51-53; tannery 25; taxi company 60; tea 68; tobacco 23, 146; trade 22, 23, 52, 67; watchmaking 52, 56; weaving 23, 27, 53; wheelwright 67; wholesale pharmaceutical department 60

history of 17, 20, 51, 143, 145, 147, 149, 150, 151, 152, 153, 154, 156, 157, 158, 159, 161

pietistic spirit of 143, 144, 159

problems of: against commerce and trade 21, 47, 49; aristocracy vs. trade 144; business too closely connected with mission 59; climate 31; communalism 27-29; credit system 47, 49, 50, 61; financial success 28; government involvement 61ff.; great stations 69; hostility of whites 39-41; opposition to large manufacturing 26, 133; secularization 29; slavery 36

successes of: economic activities supported missionaries 30, 38; people trained in thrift and order 46, 49

tensions between mission and economic activity 23, 24, 28-30, 33, 74

Morawiese Broederkerk in die Westelike Kaapprovinsie 67

Mortimer, Benjamin 40, 151

Motel, H. 143

Mott, John R. 16, 114, 166

Müller, Daniel 80

Müller, Karl 144, 148, 149, 152, 158, 159

Namasu Ltd. 140
National Council of Churches of Christ, U.S.A. 141
Nazareth 25, 27, 38
Neill, Stephen 100
Netherlands 61, 62, 158
Netherlands Antilles 60
Nettur 122
Newfoundland 44, 49, 50
New Gnadenhütten 41
New Guinea 140
New York 39, 56, 60, 148, 151
Nicaragua 27, 36, 62
Nigeria 122, 168
Nitschmann, David 18, 31, 158
North American Indians 27, 39-44, 112, 137
North Carolina 158
North German Mission Society 14
Norway 14
Nürnberg 53

Oehler, Theodore 91, 125
Ohio 41
oikoumene 64
Okak 48
Oldham, J. H. 113, 114, 116, 119, 166
Olivier, Lord 166

Palliser, Sir Hugh 44
Paraguay 39, 68, 112
Paramaribo 52-54, 60, 62, 154, 155
Paris 160
Parsons, T. 148
Paulus-Fond 168
Peacock, F. W. 152
Pelikan, Jaroslav 141
Pennsylvania 25, 151
Persia 27
Peter 156
Pfleiderer, C. 110
Pfleiderer, Gottlob 84, 90, 101, 103
Philadelphia 33
Pietism 17, 26, 134, 159
Pilgerhuth 54, 73
Pittsburgh 41
plantations 31, 35, 36, 52, 56, 57, 68, 84, 85, 97

Plebst, Georg 86, 89, 160
Pless, Count 31
Plütschau, Heinrich 14, 17, 18
Portugal 17, 51
Preiswerk, Eduard 104, 105, 163, 164, 169
Preiswerk-Imhoff, Wilhelm 111, 116, 120
Presbyterians 158
Provincial Elders' Conference of the Moravian Church in America 157

Quarshie, Tetteh 97
Quilandy 91

Raaflaub, Fritz 163
Ralfs, Marcus 51, 52, 61
Rauch, Heinrich 29
Reformation 141
Reibungsfläche 129
Reindorf, Carl Christian 169
Reynier 73
Rhenish Mission Society 14, 69
rich Christians 126, 139
Riedlingen 162
Riggenbach, C. J. 109, 161, 162, 163, 164, 168, 169
Riis, Andreas 94
Roberts, Lord 88
Roman Catholic 17, 45, 51, 90, 151, 156, 158
Rome 131
Rösinger 88, 101
Rossel, Jacques 129
Rottmann, Hermann 96, 98, 116, 128
Royal Prussian Trading Company 56
Rule of Benedict 147
Russia 14, 27, 81, 82, 160

Saalwaechter 154
Salem 41, 158
Salzmann 18
Sanskrit 160
San Thome 97
Sarasin, Karl 96, 101, 102
Surinam (Dutch Guiana) 27, 36, 51-54, 56-61, 63, 72, 73
Saxony 14, 17

Schekomeko 39, 151

Schlatter, Wilhelm 101, 131, 159, 160, 161, 162, 163, 164, 165, 166, 168, 169

Schmidt, Georg 66, 156

Schooneveld, Cornelis H. Van 145

Schott, Otto 85, 108-110, 124, 125, 131, 133

Schrenk, Elias 99, 100, 112

Schulze, Adolf 48, 153, 154, 155, 156, 157, 158

Schusha 82

secular 31, 38, 131, 140

secularization 29, 30, 137, 138, 141

Selborne, Earl of 116

Seminarium Orientale 144

Serampore Trio 158

Sessler, Jacob John 147, 148

Severin, Jacob 75

Short, Frank 119, 120, 167, 168

Siberia 158

slavery 35, 36, 42, 52, 56-59, 66, 69, 75, 98, 108, 150, 152

Society for the Furtherance of the Gospel (S.F.G.) 45-47, 49, 157

Society for the Propagation of the Gospel 153, 158

"souls for the Lamb" 33, 35

South Africa 27, 36, 67, 68, 85, 156, 157

South America 27, 39, 42, 51, 72, 97

Southey, Robert 148

South Kanara 169

Southwark, Lord Bishop of 120

Spain 17, 51

Spangenberg, August Gottlieb 22, 36, 146, 147, 149, 150, 152

Spittler, Christian Friedrich 159

Stähelin, F. 145, 153, 154

St. Croix 31, 43, 152

St. Louis 169

Stocker, F. P. 157

St. Paul 32, 64

St. Petersburg 82

"Streiteridee" 149

St. Thomas 18, 19, 31, 35, 36, 57, 144, 150

Stach, Matthias 44

Stevenson, Adlai 93

Süd-Afrika West Handel 62

Surinam 146, 153

Swedish mission 158

Switzerland 80, 89, 156, 169, 170

Tanganyika 68, 155

Tank, Nils Otto 57

Telford, John 147

Templetown, Viscount 116, 118-120

tent-making 28, 64, 72

Thames 153

Theile, Paul A. 152, 156

Thirty-nine Articles 159

Thomas, T. S. 165

Thompson, Augustus C. 149, 150, 156

Thun 79

Tiflis 82

Tolstoy 145

Trading Company 165, 168, 169

Tübingen 160

Tukuyu 68

Udipi Municipal Council 169

Ulrich, Anton 18

Ungava Bay 49

Union Trading Company 116, 121, 122, 128

Unitas Fratrum 14ff., 104, 133, 134

United Africa Company 169

United States 71

Urdu 160

Urlsperger, Johann August 80, 159

Utrecht 56

Uttendörfer, Otto 20, 144, 145, 146, 147, 150, 156

Van Calker, E. 157

Versailles Treaty 113, 114, 118

Volz, Paul 168

Volz, Peter 148

Von Campenhausen, Hans 150

Wachovian Brethren Society 158

Wagner, Hans 24, 143, 145, 146, 149

Wanner, Gustav Adolf 64, 101, 112, 159, 160, 161, 162, 163, 164, 165, 166, 167

Waso Ltd. 140

Waterloo 79
Weber, Georg 144
Weber, Max 30, 148
Wechquadnach or Indian Pond 39, 151
Weinlick, John R. 144, 149
Weiss, Jonas Paul 53, 58, 74, 154
Wesley, John 24, 30, 148
Wesleyan Methodists 162
Wesleyan mission 69
West Africa 98
West Germany 146
West Indies 14, 18, 27, 35, 162
Whitney, Eli 42
Williamson, H. Anthony 152
Winkler 80
Witschi, Hermann 161, 165, 166
World Missionary Conference-Edinburgh 113, 116, 130
Württemberg 80, 81, 86, 126, 146
Würz, Friedrich 165, 168, 170

Zamorin 90
Zander 154
Zaremba, Felician 160
Zeisberger, David 38-41, 112, 137, 151

Zeist 62
Zeister Synode 145
Zeist Mission Society 59, 157
Zellweger, Ulrich 103, 104, 108-110
Zendingstichting der Evangelischen Broederuniteit 62
Zeugengnade 136, 144
Ziegenbalg, Bartholomäus 14, 17, 18
Zimmermann, P. 165
Zinzendorf, Nikolaus Ludwig Count 14, 17-36, 43, 44, 74, 138, 144, 149, 158

   attitudes on: colonization 32, 43, 152; Eastern Church 143, 144; economic involvement 18, 19, 28, 33; education of slaves 35; financial matters 20, 23; Indians and Negroes 51; labor of missionaries 32, 33; pietism 144; trade and commerce 145; "tropes" 159

   estate, founding of 17; mission interest, history of 18; offerings 32, 33, 34; trade and commerce 21, 22, 27, 33, 74, 138

Zoar 48

DATE DUE